Viewer Discretion Advised

# Viewer Discretion Advised

*Taking Control of Mass Media Influences*

Jeffrey McCall

ROWMAN & LITTLEFIELD PUBLISHERS, INC.
Lanham • Boulder • New York • Toronto • Plymouth, UK

ROWMAN & LITTLEFIELD PUBLISHERS, INC.

Published in the United States of America
by Rowman & Littlefield Publishers, Inc.
A wholly owned subsidiary of The Rowman & Littlefield Publishing Group, Inc.
4501 Forbes Boulevard, Suite 200, Lanham, Maryland 20706
www.rowmanlittlefield.com

Estover Road, Plymouth PL6 7PY, United Kingdom

British Library Cataloguing in Publication Information Available

**Library of Congress Cataloging-in-Publication Data**
McCall, Jeffrey M. (Jeffrey Michael), 1954–
    Viewer discretion advised : taking control of mass media influences / Jeffrey
McCall.
  p. cm.
  Includes bibliographical references and index.
  ISBN-13: 978-0-7425-5519-8 (cloth : alk. paper)
  ISBN-10: 0-7425-5519-4 (cloth : alk. paper)
  ISBN-13: 978-0-7425-5520-4 (pbk. : alk. paper)
  ISBN-10: 0-7425-5520-8 (pbk. : alk. paper)
  1. Mass media—United States. 2. Mass media—Influence. I. Title.
P92.U5M37 2007
302.2'30973—dc22

                                              2006101414

Printed in the United States of America

 ♾️™ The paper used in this publication meets the minimum requirements of
American National Standard for Information Sciences—Permanence of Paper
for Printed Library Materials, ANSI/NISO Z39.48-1992.

# Contents

# Preface and Acknowledgments

It has always seemed odd that the study of mass media is so overlooked in our society. Clearly, the media influence our lives in so many ways and on a daily basis. The media affect our cultural values, economy, political system, and even how we use our free time. Yet, even at many universities, the study of the media is reserved largely for training future broadcasters and journalists. At institutions where the media are studied more broadly as a liberal arts discipline, the departments are generally not supported or respected. In fact, a number of our nation's prominent universities have no formal media studies programs at all. Our nation is worse off because our citizenry is not informed enough about how the media work and their impact.

After working for several years in the media world, I decided to teach college students about how the media function in our society. That has been a rewarding vocation. College students are eager to study the media because they are so involved with mediated messages on a constant basis. They want to know how to analyze and interpret those messages and the institutions that develop them. Students frequently comment at the end of a semester studying broadcast news or media culture that they can no longer just "watch television." They now critique and scrutinize the messages as they receive them. These students have developed some degree of media literacy.

Even college professors who are dedicated to the classroom, however, only reach a relatively small number of students. My interest in reaching more people to discuss the media prompted me to look into avenues beyond the classroom.

Larry Anderson, of my university's public relations office, suggested I write newspaper opinion columns for general readership. Over the last several years, my columns have appeared in a number of newspapers around the country, covering a wide range of issues. I have written about the FCC's regulatory efforts to manage indecent content. I have written about the news agenda that is shaped by broadcast news producers. Other topics have included the impact of television on kids, the regulation of media ownership, how the First Amendment functions, and the role of the media in our nation's politics.

The columns have been read by producers in the electronic media and led to television and radio appearances. On other occasions, newspaper writers covering these issues have followed up with published interviews, thus furthering the dialogue on these important topics. After almost every column or broadcast interview, I receive e-mails, letters, and/or phone calls from people who indicate that the perspectives shared provide them a new or different outlook. Of course, they don't necessarily always agree with the perspective presented, but it's good that they have assessed the issue in a manner they might not otherwise have.

This book is designed to further the discussion of those media issues that I have determined are of most interest and utility to American citizens, based on the feedback I have received in recent years from students, readers, and viewers. The presentation includes perspectives and analyses that are designed to encourage readers to think about the issues. Most of all, it is hoped that readers will feel empowered by learning more about the media and take an active role in managing their own media consumption. Further, it is hoped that readers will actively assert their priorities and wishes to the editors and producers who frame the content of our nation's media.

I want to acknowledge the many people who have been instrumental and helpful in my career and in the development of this book.

I am grateful for the superb instruction and guidance I received during my undergraduate and graduate education. As an undergraduate at DePauw University, and then later as a faculty colleague, I benefited a great deal from the guidance of Professors Robert Weiss and Larry Sutton. At the University of Illinois, Professors Kurt Ritter and Ellen Ritter were inspiring teachers and mentors. At the University of Missouri, Professor Michael Porter was a great role model and excellent teacher as he guided my doctoral program. Also at Mizzou, I benefited from the insights of journalism professor Elmer Lower, the former president of ABC News, who was a key leader in the development of ABC as a force in electronic journalism.

I appreciate the discussions and cooperation of Larry Anderson and Ken Owen of the DePauw public relations office. My department's office manager, Joyce Christiansen, is always helpful and cooperative. The professional dialogue and collaborations I've enjoyed with Bill Christ of Trinity University and Paul Gullifor of Bradley University have been very helpful over the years. At the *Indianapolis Star*, I thank Focus editor Jane Lichtenberg for her support.

From Rowman & Littlefield, I thank acquisitions editor Brenda Hadenfeldt, assistant editor Bess Vanrenen, and production editor Janice Braunstein. They have been most helpful at each step in the process.

On a personal note, I thank my sons Pete, Kevin, and Steve for their love and support of my writing. Pete was among the first people to suggest that I expand on the topics covered in my op-eds and put them in a book.

I owe so very much to my parents, Don McCall and the late Rita McCall, for instilling in me and my siblings—Peggy, Skip, and Fred—the value of education and the importance of independent thinking. I am grateful for their love and guidance. They worked hard and sacrificed much to make sure their kids had the best educational opportunities.

Most of all, I thank my wife, Cathy, whom I love deeply. She is my best friend. She is also my first sounding board and editor for all writing topics. Her support and encouragement for this project, and, indeed, throughout the years, have been much appreciated.

# CHAPTER ONE

⨋

# Media Awareness for All

A television set is on for nearly eight hours in the average American home each day, with each occupant viewing something on television for nearly four hours daily. The average American listens to radio over three hours each day. Add video games, Internet browsing, DVD watching, occasional movie attendance, and roadside billboards to this equation, and it is clear that Americans are deluged with mediated messages in every waking moment. By now, media use (and misuse) is just an accepted aspect of American culture, as people have become protoplasmic blobs being washed over by countless messages that seek to alter your political views, make you buy something, or change your values. These narcotizing messages seek to keep you watching so that your eyeballs can be sold to advertisers. Media usage has become more than a supplement to our American lifestyle; it has become perhaps the largest aspect of our lifestyle. More productive pursuits like exercise, family interaction, community work, and household duties are overlooked in order to keep up with *American Idol* or catch the big ball game on TV. For most Americans, time spent with the media surpasses time spent at work or at sleep, and certainly surpasses human interaction with friends and family.

More alarming, perhaps, than simply how much the media intrude on and impact American lives, however, is the low level of insight and awareness people bring to their media-consuming habits. Americans are generally ignorant of how the media operate and the potential impact of mediated messages. Americans operate at a low level of awareness about how news decisions are made, how the media are financed, how the government regulates the media (or doesn't), the impact of advertising, the role of the media in political decisions, and so on.

This ignorance is caused, in part, by our nation's education system, which has failed to acknowledge the media's elephant in society's living room. From kindergarten through college, the American education system strives to enlighten students about those aspects of the world that affect or enrich their lives. The rationale is that American citizens need the empowerment that comes from being made functional in math, the scientific world, speaking and writing the English language, computers, civics, and the arts. Schools from the primary level through college even have curricula designed to show people how to get along with each other, resolve conflicts, and develop tolerance. Indeed, today's educational programs seek to develop well-rounded individuals who can understand the basics of their surroundings and be prepared to engage the world on their own terms.

Remarkably missing from the essential understandings list, however, is any widespread educational initiative to help Americans engage a force that impacts them daily and affects their worldviews on everything from fashion to health to social standards to international affairs. Thus, the formal education system, in its narrow-sightedness, leaves the average American largely ignorant about the mass media world, how it operates, and how it affects his or her daily life. So, students at almost every level of their education program will learn how to read and write poetry, for example, even though virtually none of them will ever read or write poetry outside of a school setting. The media, however, which will surround a person's daily lifestyle, are left unstudied.

While some media literacy standards have made it into the educational programs of many states, the relevant content is usually buried in language arts or social studies classes and taught by teachers whose specialties are in literature or history. In such cases, mention of the media is parenthetical to whatever other subject matter is being discussed.

The media industry itself must also be blamed for this societal ignorance of how the media world works. Ever their own sacred cows, media power brokers, appear to like keeping the public unaware of the media industry's workings. As long as media consumers are conditioned to just unquestioningly take whatever mediated messages come down the pike, producers and programmers more easily escape accountability. Why would the media industry feel compelled to enlighten consumers about media ratings practices, setting the news agenda, regulatory practices, corporate ownership circumstances, and so forth, when doing so might actually spark citizens to question what they receive and even challenge it? Media coverage of itself, when it happens, frequently is self-congratulatory, self-promotional, or pop culture based. Newspapers do movie reviews and report the antics of media personalities. Television stations do "news" stories about the premieres of new sitcoms or the latest *Survivor* development. Serious coverage of the media industry, however, is segregated only to industry trade magazines where the public is not likely to know of corporate media economic trends, changes in federal oversight, technological advances, or editorial and content decision making. Although some newspapers have moved forward with columns that help audiences understand the decisions of the paper, for the most part, if an average media consumer wants to know anything about the media's operation and impact, she or he should not look to the popular media outlets to find it. Clearly, media decision makers and producers maintain a high degree of power when they shield consumers from understanding how mediated messages work and the power of media corporations.

The American public, however, must shoulder its share of the blame for failing to understand how the media operate and for not necessarily caring about this apparent ignorance. Americans expect to know about the inside goings-on of their favorite sports teams or musicians, and will update themselves on new appliances and technical gizmos, but they have little interest in the workings of the organizations that determine the content of their entertainment and topics for their news. Indeed, Americans are not active when it comes to learning about and holding the media accountable.

Every red-blooded American will return spoiled food to the grocer for a refund or a replacement. Bad service at a restaurant gets a protest to the manager. If you buy a car that doesn't function as it should, you take it back with the expectation that it will be replaced or made functional.

But while everybody has engaged in this kind of consumer action, it is rare for media consumers to express their disapproval to the general managers of television or radio stations, or the editors of newspapers. Prior to the Janet Jackson Super Bowl "wardrobe malfunction," the Federal Communications Commission (FCC) routinely only received about thirty complaints per month about indecent content on the radio and television airwaves. The FCC now receives hundreds and sometimes thousands of complaints per month, but even most of those are mass-generated by media watchdog groups hoping to capitalize on the attention of the Super Bowl faux pas. National surveys show that over half of Americans are concerned about indecent content in broadcasting, but that sentiment is hardly reflected in the modest citizen actions.

Public contacts to the media, when made, are generally not substantive. People who call radio stations are usually trying to win a prize, request a song, or suggest that the local baseball team's manager be canned. Callers to television stations are more likely to critique the anchorwoman's latest hairdo than question news content. Letters to the editor of the newspaper are more likely designed to comment about a local issue or politician than scrutinize the newspaper's performance.

The public has bought in to the frequent refrain of media management to external criticism. The media biggies say that if you don't like what's on the radio or TV, turn the dial. If you don't like the newspaper, don't read it. Too often, public criticism is viewed by media execs as self-serving rants from commoners who don't know anything about the media and are in no position to judge, or that somehow, public criticism is an attempt to censor and infringe on the media's free press rights. A comprehensive study of plaintiffs who filed libel suits several years ago revealed that most filers only went to court after receiving the brush-off from news executives who ignored the complaint or dismissed it as not worthy of consideration. The public has as much (or more?) right to expect high performance from their media outlets as they do their food suppliers, appliance manufacturers, plumbers, and other service providers, but average media consumers take little initiative and feel powerless in dealing with media outlets.

Americans are heavily invested in the media in terms of both time and money. Countless hours are spent listening, watching, and reading mediated messages. Subscriptions to cable or satellite television sap our personal budgets. We sit still to watch thousands of commercials so broadcasters can bring us "free" television. Electronic reception equipment like television sets, DVD players, and stereo radios cost consumers millions each year. Yet, the public sits still while networks provide routine prime-time programming filled with sex, violence, and stupid jokes and one-liners that would not even get a chuckle at your next cocktail party. Radio stations are licensed by the FCC to serve the interests of local communities, but increasingly program music is piped in by satellite with occasional narration by a guy located a thousand miles from your town. Most radio stations now have zero public service programming and no local news, weather, or sports. And the public just turns the dial if they don't like the program, instead of demanding that the station meets its FCC mandate to "serve the public interest." Only the largest metropolitan areas now have competing newspapers. Thus, if you want to read a newspaper, you read the only option you have, regardless of whether you think it provides accurate and balanced coverage. This lack of newspaper competition surely fuels the powerless feelings of readers and the monopolistic attitude of the local publishers.

But why don't media consumers stand up for themselves and consistently provide media producers with their perspectives about the content they watch, hear, and read? Why are media consumers so unaware of the influences these messages might be having on their attitudes, values, and buying habits? It is because they don't know about the power of the messages, how the media work, or how to impact the system. Citizens have a right, even an obligation, to influence the media marketplace to more clearly reflect their interests, values, and priorities. For this to happen, however, the public needs to become more media literate.

## The Concept of Media Literacy

In 1992, some thirty communication educators and scholars met under the sponsorship of the Aspen Institute to discuss the need for making Americans more media literate. They described media literacy as a movement to help "people understand, produce and negotiate meanings in a culture made up of powerful images, words and sounds." They explained that the media must be studied from the standpoint of how messages are constructed and how those messages define reality for the viewing public. They further suggested that the media's commercial implications must be understood, along with the ideological and political implications. While all of this sounds a bit "educratic," the basic gist is on target that media consumers need better insight to where mass messages are coming from, how they affect our broader and personal economic interests, and what effects they might be having on our societal views.

The conferees acknowledged the many challenges facing the kick-start of a formal media literacy initiative in school systems. Those challenges still largely exist today, from funding to curricular materials to training of current teachers. The major obstacle, however, could well be the bias against popular media as not being worthy of study and serious academic attention. While it is generally okay to use the media in teaching other subjects, academic snootyism suggests that it is not legitimate to teach *about* the media.

Communication researcher Jim Potter of the University of California–Santa Barbara says, "The purpose of media literacy is to empower individuals to control media programming." He is not speaking here of controlling what media organizations actually program and disseminate to us (although that also is possible in an indirect sense), he is speaking of "control over the way one's mind gets programmed" by the media. Through media literacy, media consumers are empowered to make sensible choices and understand the media's effects, becoming more active participants in the communication process and not merely absorbing messages like stereotypical couch potatoes. As Potter writes, "The more you are aware of how the media operate and how they affect you, the more you gain control over those effects, and the more you will separate yourself from typical media users who have turned over a great deal of their lives to the media without realizing it." Media literacy scholar James A. Brown writes, "Critically perceiving and thinking about these mediated experiences is central to being 'educated' and to how we live."

FCC commissioner Michael Copps has emerged as a leading advocate for the public's interests in media regulation. In a speech in June 2006, Copps pointed out "the media literacy gap in our nation's educational curriculum" and called for a K–12 media literacy program "to teach kids not only how to use the media but how the media uses them."

There have been isolated pockets of progress in promoting media literacy in the United States. Still, the United States, with its citizens undoubtedly barraged by more media choices and messages each day compared to other nations, lags behind the world in media education. Media literacy curricula are more developed and widespread in numerous countries, including Australia, where primary and secondary media education has been required for a decade, as well as Great Britain, Israel, Canada, and others.

Several organizations and think tanks have helped fuel the media literacy movement by creating websites, providing sample curricula, and promoting the importance of the media literacy idea. The New Mexico Media Literacy Project is one of the more successful of these organizations, along with the Center for Media Literacy and the Alliance for a Media Literate America. Others have a more ideological agenda but still have contributions to make in helping Americans understand the media. For example, the Action Coalition for Media Education focuses largely on the media as capitalistic enterprises that promote unnecessary consumerism and inappropriate gender and racial portrayals. The National Institute on Media and the Family is concerned with the decay of mainstream family values and the immorality imposed by the entertainment industry. Sadly, however, many curriculum planners at local schools and even colleges have never heard of any of these media literacy groups. Further, there is virtually no federal or state educational funding specifically for media literacy programs in schools.

The American Academy of Pediatrics has called for media literacy curricula for children and adolescents to teach them how to critically assess mediated messages, particularly of advertising. The academy believes that media education "seems to be protective in mitigating harmful effects of media, including the effects of cigarette, alcohol and food advertising."

Colleges and universities, like primary and secondary schools, have done little to further the cause of media literacy. The study of the media is reserved largely for those students who are studying to enter media or media-related careers. Departments of mass communication and/or journalism provide for little enrollment from students in the sciences, liberal arts, or business, so media awareness is only deemed necessary for future media practitioners. General education requirements at colleges demand that students are exposed to foreign language, the arts, science, multiculturalism, and so on, but not necessarily to the media forces that will shape their worldviews, impact their businesses, and help to raise their kids. Many top-tier colleges have no academic departments devoted to the study of media, although they might have some courses scattered in political science, English, or sociology departments that allow for media bashing within broader ideological discussions.

The seeds of media literacy awareness are emerging at some major universities. The Peabody Center for Media and Society at the University of Georgia has issued a seminar report expressing the need to prepare media-literate citizens to participate in today's world. The Manship School of Mass Communication at Louisiana State University (LSU) recently created the first endowed faculty chair in the nation focused on media literacy. LSU dean John Maxwell Hamilton said the initiative demonstrates the increasing "need to equip Americans to understand how to distinguish responsible journalism and advertising." The accompanying program intends to push LSU to the forefront in teaching non–mass communication students how to analyze the media.

## Media Literacy Fake-Outs

Some initiatives that would appear to help empower citizens in their media awareness are actually little more than shallow hype, or worse, self-serving diversions from the real problems of the media. The annual TV-Turnoff Week, for example, shows up each spring with its gimmicky message to just turn the television off for a week. The message here is that TV is the "idiot box," "boob tube," and "plug-in drug." Painting television as evil, however, and encouraging people to simply do a Lenten-style fast for a week sends a distorted message that television itself is the problem, rather than the improper manner in which we overuse television. A major problem with this campaign is that the TV gets turned off from those programs that are actually redeeming. In addition, many families who take this campaign seriously feel good about their one-week television fast, then simply resume their previous viewing habits.

The National Cable and Telecommunications Association (NCTA) rolled out its "Take Control. It's Easy" campaign in 2005 with the false appearance it was interested in helping empower families in choosing the programs they viewed. The campaign told parents to pay more attention to the on-screen ratings systems, and to use the V-chips in their television sets to block out undesirable programming. The underlying message was that the cable television industry had no responsibility for television content. Overlooked in all of this was the fact that most viewers don't understand the on-screen ratings and don't have their V-chips activated. Further, many kids don't have parents who "take control," or who have the technical savvy to bypass the V-chips. In addition, the Parents Television Council reports that some edgy programs are inaccurately labeled for ratings purposes. Clearly, campaigns like this one of the NCTA and other such broadcaster-sponsored on-air "awareness" campaigns do little to address media literacy and merely wash the industry's hands of responsibility.

## Media Literacy for the Masses

Ample evidence indicates that media consumers can be made more literate when they are provided insights to how the media function. Potter cites many examples of studies that demonstrate that media consumers can be made more aware of media processes and, thus, empowered. This book is designed to provide some of that media awareness for those consumers who want greater insights on the key media issues of the day. Average media consumers need to know more about how "news" gets defined by producers and editors, and whether that news agenda, as determined by those editors, tells us what is really important for us. Citizens need to know how the First Amendment, which guarantees free expression, is often mischaracterized and warped by various public leaders and the media. The process through which the FCC oversees electronic media is poorly understood by most listeners and viewers, thus leaving them less capable of impacting the system to hold the FCC and broadcasters accountable. Changes in ownership and corporate structures have altered the media landscape in recent years and have reduced the ability of media to serve *local* audiences. These ownership changes have hardly been covered or explained by the mainstream press. Other key issues in today's media content involve the role of the media in political elections, the pervasiveness of media in kids' lives, and the need for regular citizens to impact media decisions by proactively letting producers and editors know the public's priorities and values. This book provides insights on these and other issues, all to guide media consumers to take charge of their media-consuming habits and to get involved in demanding that media outlets serve us more effectively.

# CHAPTER TWO

∽

# Getting to Know
# the First Amendment

Perhaps no segment of the Constitution is more misunderstood in American society than the First Amendment. Many people incorrectly assume the concept of free expression means that anybody can say anything about any subject in any place at any time and without any repercussions. Of course, as the Supreme Court has instructed over the years, the Constitution doesn't protect free speech in all circumstances and doesn't protect the speakers from the consequences of their speech. Communication, indeed, is limited by the courts in those circumstances in which there is a compelling governmental or societal interest. You wouldn't know that from the free speech absolutists who believe there should be no restrictions on their messages . . . but usually don't mind limitations on voices they don't like.

Even professional media types, who in many ways benefit the most from the freedoms provided in the First Amendment, on occasion help to create the surrounding confusion with misguided assertions. For example, in October 2005, the Media Institute and the National Association of Broadcasters Educational Foundation created a public service announcement to lend support to Freedom of Speech Week. The announcement proclaimed, "Freedom of Speech: There is a reason it's the First Amendment." The assertion, of course, was that the amendment was ranked first by the Constitution's framers to signal its preeminence. Although the concept of free expression was, indeed, quite important to the founding fathers, it was also highly controversial—enough so that the freedoms contained in the First Amendment were not included in the original constitution. Note that freedom of speech, press, religion, and so on, as provided in the First Amendment, were concepts added in an *amendment* to the original constitution. Further—and here's the surprise for many media professionals—the First Amendment was actually third in a list of twelve amendments sent by President George Washington to the states for ratification in 1789. The first two amendments on the list, which dealt with the number of members in the House of Representatives and the process for raising congressional salaries, were never ratified. Thus, the reason the freedoms contained in the First Amendment are in the *first* amendment is that these other two amendments didn't survive the ratification process.

The First Amendment is quite remarkable in its directness, brevity, and impact: "Congress shall make no law respecting an establishment of religion, or prohibiting the free exercise thereof; or abridging the freedom of speech, or of the press, or the right of the people peaceably to assemble, and to petition the Government for redress of grievances." These few words have created the framework in which generations of Americans have been allowed to express themselves freely and hold the government accountable for its actions.

Sadly, too many Americans are not aware of the freedoms guaranteed in the First Amendment or have little understanding of what the freedoms are designed to accomplish. Surveys abound to demonstrate this disturbing ignorance of the constitutional principles that, in many ways, characterize American democracy.

A survey conducted by the McCormick Tribune Freedom Museum in 2006 raised eyebrows with its finding that barely a fourth of Americans could name at least two of the five freedoms guaranteed in the First Amendment, but over half of all Americans could name at least two members of *The Simpsons* cartoon family. The average American can also name more of the *American Idol* judges than freedoms provided in the First Amendment. Only 69 percent of Americans could name freedom of speech as guaranteed in the First Amendment and only 11 percent could name freedom of the press. Shockingly, 27 percent of those surveyed could not name a single freedom of the First Amendment.

Those results are consistent with a 2005 study conducted by the First Amendment Center, with 63 percent of respondents in the survey being able to identify freedom of speech as a guaranteed freedom of the First Amendment and 16 percent identifying freedom of the press. Almost 40 percent of the public think the press has too much freedom, and over half believe citizens should be prohibited from saying things in public that might be offensive to a racial or religious group. And it doesn't stop there. Twenty-six percent of Americans strongly disagree with the statement "Newspapers should be allowed to freely criticize the U.S. military about its strategy and performance," and 12 percent mildly agree with that statement. Constitutional framers would cringe at such public disregard for the fundamental freedoms they worked so hard to guarantee.

A Knight Foundation study of high school students also found disappointing and shocking results. More than a third of the one hundred thousand students surveyed agreed with the statement "The First Amendment goes too far in the rights it guarantees," *after* being presented with the actual wording of the amendment. Only 51 percent believe newspapers should be allowed to publish freely without government approval of stories, and 32 percent believe the press has too much freedom. But while many high schoolers think the First Amendment goes too far in insuring freedom and are OK with the government approving newspaper stories, 70 percent defend the rights of musicians to perform songs with offensive lyrics. Knight Foundation president Hodding Carter III responded to these results with alarm: "These results are not only disturbing; they are dangerous. Ignorance about the basics of this free society is a danger to our nation's future."

Carter is correct, of course. The liberty of any society is directly connected to the values and commitments of the citizens. A society that doesn't understand its freedoms or takes them for granted is susceptible to losing those freedoms. Citizens who don't see the benefit of a free press, or worse, are comfortable with government restrictions on that press, won't be available to apply public pressure should those press freedoms come under assault. Those naïve people who figure that the courts will always be there to protect constitutional liberties fail to note that courts are highly responsive to the social pressures of the time, and that judges are appointed by politicians who are even more directly responsive to social pressure, or lack thereof.

Our nation's education system usually gets the blame for this obviously dim awareness of the country's liberties. Some blame is well deserved. Too many high schools, and even colleges, have deemphasized study of America's founding principles in favor of devoting more time to self-actualization, pop culture, tolerance, and so on. These other areas for "study" might well have some uses, but not at the expense of the society's foundational principles. Further, the ability to self-actualize and an understanding of tolerance emanate largely from the kinds of liberties provided in the First Amendment, but those connections are nowhere to be made. For various reasons the insights of First Amendment framers like James Madison and Thomas Jefferson are viewed as unnecessary, outdated, irrelevant footnotes. At colleges, the curriculums in many history departments feature more courses on world history, Asian history, South American history, and so forth than courses in United States history.

The media, themselves, must shoulder the largest burden of blame for the nation's low level of awareness of First Amendment issues. No institution, including the government, has more direct opportunity to influence and educate Americans than the mass media system. No institution has been entrusted more by the First Amendment itself to freely operate in disseminating information and ideas to the citizenry. The media, however, have failed to fully live up to their potential to enlighten the public about many issues, the value of free expression high among them.

Allowed to operate freely and as money-making institutions, the media collectively have too often been sidetracked to worry first about profits, ratings, entertainment, and sideshows, and only in a secondary sense about fueling the conversation of democracy in a way that would create public awareness and appreciation for the free flow of ideas. Poor performance by the media hardly makes the public want to rally around press freedoms. Various polls demonstrate that public confidence in newspapers and television news operations has fallen. A majority of the public believes news outlets often report inaccurately, try to cover up mistakes, and are too profit driven and biased. Beyond that, the media frequently act as their own sacred cow, seldom engaging in responsible self-critique, pointing fingers at demagogues but not doing sufficient introspection. The media fail to sensibly explain the proper role of the press and citizens in living out the First Amendment's promise. Media-sponsored First Amendment crusades are too often focused on self-pitying battles for information from government offices, trying to avoid subpoenas, or in the case of broadcasters, pushing the envelope for the "rights" to broadcast indecent content on publicly owned airwaves. When the media's free speech role models are the likes of shock radio jock Howard Stern, the *New York Times*'s Judith Miller, and CBS Super Bowl producers defending wardrobe malfunctions, it is little wonder the public doesn't understand the broader importance of mediated free expression and won't rally for First Amendment principles, even at its own ultimate expense.

## The Framers' Commitment to Free Expression

The constitutional framers saw the importance of providing the citizenry with freedoms of speech, religion, and press, largely because of their beliefs that these were basic human liberties. They also believed that free expression ultimately led to the discovery of truth and for the effective operation of a government system in which power resided in the citizenry. The free press was deemed to be an essential component of these overall liberties because it was believed the colonial press had been instrumental in fueling debate before and during the struggle for independence. In addition, the press could take on the role of surrogate of the public, gathering and distributing information in ways that individual citizens could hardly do on their own. Thus, the press could serve as a watchdog of the government, on behalf of the public, keeping public officials accountable for their actions and keeping citizens aware of government performance.

America became the ideal place for a commitment to free expression to develop because it was being settled by independent-minded dreamers who realized the need for interdependence. They could assure their own freedom to exercise religion, publish, and speak by allowing others to have theirs.

James Madison is widely regarded as the key thinker and organizer of the First Amendment. He initiated the discussions in the House of

Representatives that eventually created the initial batch of constitutional amendments, including what became the First Amendment. It is believed he drew largely from language in the Pennsylvania Constitution, which already provided for free speech and a free press. Madison and his close friend and political ally Thomas Jefferson worked hard to craft the language of the First Amendment and shepherd it through the congressional approval and eventual ratification process. Free expression skeptics at the time warned about the potential for free press rights to be abused. Madison answered by saying, "Some degree of abuse is inseparable from the proper use of everything; and in no instance is this more true than that of the press." In essence, Madison argued that the potential abuses had to be tolerated in order to get the benefits a free press would provide, namely, the knowledge the citizenry could attain as they strived for self-governance.

## Protected and Unprotected Expression

Even with a constitutional provision to protect free speech and press, not all expression is actually "protected." Over the years, the courts and communication theorists have tried to sort out what kinds of messages are constitutionally protected and which ones should not be. Only the most extreme absolutist would endorse a communication free-for-all in which there are absolutely no legal or social restraints on communicators. Of course, the challenge is in finding the proper balance of allowing the free flow of ideas and expression, yet shielding society from messages that could well harm it. Theorists have worked over the years to distinguish worthwhile expression, which serves a political or social interest and should obviously be protected by the courts, from worthless speech, which does not serve a public purpose. This is not an easy task and has led to much debate and splitting of hairs.

It is absolutely clear, however, that the courts have never interpreted the First Amendment as an absolutist statement in which any and all communication is to be allowed. Supreme Court justice William Brennan, one of our nation's most powerful and articulate defenders of free expression, wrote in a 1957 decision that "it is apparent that the unconditional phrasing of the First Amendment was not intended to protect every utterance." Brennan went on to quote an earlier Supreme

Court opinion written by Justice Frank Murphy, which said, "There are certain well-defined and narrowly limited classes of speech, the prevention and punishment of which have never thought to raise any Constitutional problem. . . . It has been well observed that such utterances are no essential part of any exposition of ideas, and are of such slight social value as a step to truth that any benefit that may be derived from them is clearly outweighed by the social interest in order and morality."

Obscenity is one of those classes of communication that is not protected by the First Amendment. Although absolutists and the many people who make money in the world of obscenity defend its production, it can be argued that obscene messages serve no worthwhile purpose and, in all likelihood, harm the society. Laws against obscenity are on the books, and the courts have consistently ruled that obscene messages are not protected speech. Defining obscenity, however, is the tricky part of the equation. The courts have tried to provide guidance to government prosecutors over the years, and the Supreme Court's *Miller* test has provided the steps to be taken in determining what material is legally obscene. The first step in determining whether material is obscene is to decide whether the material in question, taken as a whole, is offensive to the community's standards and appeals to "prurient interests." Next, the material must describe in an offensive way sexual conduct that is illegal by state law. Such conduct would be rape, child sex offenses, and so forth. Finally, the work as a whole must be deemed to lack any serious artistic, political, or scientific value. Going through this definitional gauntlet is quite challenging for prosecutors, many of whom pass on prosecutable cases just because of the difficulty of going to trial with such subjective definitional circumstances. Even though obscene communication is not constitutionally protected, it takes government prosecutors with initiative to stop the practice.

Even with the First Amendment, citizens don't have a "right" to engage in communication that could create a "clear and present danger" to the society or to incite people in a manner that would create a current likelihood of lawbreaking activity. The courts also don't protect the use of "fighting words" as free speech, the rationale being that threats and hostile name-calling could "incite an immediate breach of the peace," and make no contribution to sensible discussion of ideas.

The courts also allow governments to restrict parades, protests, and demonstrations on occasion based on what are known as "time, place, and manner" restrictions. In these matters, free speech can't be closed off altogether, but the expressions can be channeled in ways that suit the greater needs of a community. For example, a city can choose to not allow noisy parades late at night when they would disrupt the sleep of many citizens. A community can restrict the location of a demonstration so that it doesn't block the flow of traffic or create safety hazards. These sorts of restrictions on free expression can be complicated to craft and enforce, but they clearly demonstrate the government's interest and constitutional ability to limit free speech and that the First Amendment doesn't signal a communication free-for-all.

Another communication that is not protected as free speech is in the area of libel or slander. In these cases, a speaker can assume no right to defame or ruin the reputation of another person or group by disseminating falsehoods. Although there is no provision in law that prevents someone from making defamatory statements in the first place, the First Amendment right to free expression does not protect a speaker or writer from being punished after the fact for any harm created for the victim of the falsehoods. Defamatory messages distributed through the print or broadcast media are defined as libelous, and defamatory messages distributed through spoken communication are considered to be slander. Generally, penalties for libel are harsher than penalties for slander because the potential harm of mediated defamation is so much greater. It is important to note that defamation cases are not considered in criminal courts and are thus not prosecuted by the government. These libel and slander cases are, instead, considered as civil matters. Also of note, the Supreme Court has determined that persons who put themselves in the public eye as politicians, government officials, or even professional entertainers have a higher standard to meet in order to win a libel case. Such public persons, by being in positions of public interest, must prove that defamatory press reports about them were published with intent to harm, or with "actual malice." This allows the media to make an unintentional reporting error when covering a prominent person and not suffer from a libel suit. Private individuals, on the other hand, can win a libel suit without proving actual malice if they can demonstrate that the false reporting was the result merely of journalistic negligence. Thus, the courts say that public persons must put up with more public scrutiny, including accidental falsehoods, in exchange for their public roles.

On rare occasions, courts can restrict free speech as a means to support a defendant's Sixth Amendment right to a fair trial. A judge can issue a restrictive order, sometimes called a gag order, to keep the press from publishing information in advance of a criminal trial if the judge believes that is the only way to maintain conditions in which it's possible for the defendant to receive a fair trial. This practice is seldom used because of the importance of maintaining free press rights. In such cases, the judge must ascertain that the case is sure to receive a high degree of pretrial publicity, that stifling press reports of the matter is the only reasonable manner to ensure such publicity doesn't disrupt the potential for a fair trial, and that the order is designed to keep possible prejudicial information away from jurors. More common are restrictive orders from judges that limit in advance what participants in an upcoming trial are allowed to say in public. Judges can, in certain high-profile circumstances, prohibit trial participants like attorneys, witnesses, and police officers from commenting publicly about a trial before and during the proceedings. This was the case during the trial of Scott Peterson, who was tried for the murder of his wife, Laci, and their unborn child. Such orders, while clearly restricting free expression, are made to protect a defendant's opportunity for a fair trial and to limit the prospects of trying a case in the media.

Communicators through broadcast airwaves have limitations on their full free speech rights. For example, Congress has legislated, and the courts have upheld, requirements that broadcasters serve the "public interest, convenience, and necessity." In essence, since broadcasters are licensed by the Federal Communications Commission (FCC) to use publicly owned airwaves, they are expected to provide programs that serve the public. Although this is a standard that has been difficult to assess over the years, it is clearly a restriction on the free expression of the broadcast owners. Owners of newspapers, magazines, and so on have no such mandate that they serve the public interest. In the realm of political communication, broadcasters are required by law to provide access to their airwaves for federal candidates, and to provide equal opportunity for candidates to appear in nonnews programs or to buy political advertising time. Such rules reduce broadcasters' full free speech rights in ways that print media owners' rights are not reduced. A newspaper owner can actively promote the candidacy of one politician through editorials and even free advertising. A broadcaster, however, must keep the opportunities balanced for all candidates. Does a broadcaster have full free speech rights when he is mandated to air messages that counter his original comments in support of a political candidate? In addition, the government, through the FCC, can legally restrict who can acquire a broadcast license in the first place. Citizens are not entitled to expression over broadcast airwaves, and the FCC will award licenses only to prospective owners who have no criminal background, have the financial resources to adequately operate the station, and will commit to serving the public interest. The entire licensing process is indeed a free speech restriction that is allowed by the courts. Pirate broadcasters who set up their own outlets outside of the FCC are subject to being shut down by federal marshals, fined, and possibly jailed.

The Supreme Court has also made it clear over the years that commercial speech can be regulated by the government when needed to protect the interests of consumers. The government, largely through the enforcement of the Federal Trade Commission (FTC), works to restrict false and deceptive advertising. The court has made it clear that commercial expression does not deserve the same First Amendment protection as political speech. For example, do-not-call registries to prevent phone solicitations by product marketers do not apply to political campaigns making phone calls into private homes. The FTC enforces policies that basically require commercial product messages to be truthful. (Obviously, there aren't any enforcement measures against false or deceptive political speech, as evidenced by the amount of such speech in the political arena!)

As seen in the broad areas just reviewed, even with a First Amendment, the government has maintained the power to restrict free expression in many ways, finding a middle ground between the free-for-all that would take place with an absolutist approach to free expression and the stifling atmosphere of censorship and oppression of communication.

## Misconceptions and Misapplications of Free Expression

Although most Americans pay lip service to the concept of free speech, most everybody would be happy to censor certain messages or people on occasion. A prime example came recently when the American Civil Liberties Union (ACLU) generated a proposal to prohibit its board members from publicly stating any disagreements with board policies. The ACLU, of course, prides itself on its commitment to free expression and has provided legal support on numerous occasions to uphold the free speech rights of individuals. The gag rule proposal was viewed as hypocritical by many ACLU critics. Interestingly, the ACLU, as a private organization, is free to enact such rules on its members. The First Amendment would only come into play should the government try to gag ACLU members . . . in which case the ACLU would surely sue to protect free speech rights!

The media industry postures itself as the public's defender of the First Amendment, when in reality much lobbying by media groups is designed to protect the industry and its money-making ability. The Free Speech Coalition would seem to be a professional organization seeking to protect the public's free expression rights against government oppression. Actually, the coalition represents and is funded by producers in the adult entertainment industry to fight pornography and obscenity laws, thus claiming to protect free expression for all of us. The Media Institute is a think tank funded by the nation's biggest media corporations. Its big cause has been to fight the FCC over its indecency and profanity rulings, all designed to keep the corporations from getting fined and from reeling in edgy content in broadcast radio and television. Likewise, the Center for Creative Voices fights for the rights of media outlets to creatively say and do whatever they want, regardless of federal law or community standards.

Much public confusion about the operation of the First Amendment surely develops because of cases in which high-profile organizations or personalities assert constitutional protections that don't exist. In some cases, people believe they have a right to express themselves in forums they don't control or to force people to communicate when they don't want to. There are those people who want to freely express themselves but think they should be immune from any consequences of those expressions. And then there are the free speech advocates who don't mind at all to try to stifle the communication of others. The illustrations below demonstrate how free speech principles can be misapplied.

## No Right to Access

- Heavy metal band Mötley Crüe was banned by NBC from future network appearances after a foul-mouthed performance on *The Tonight Show*. The band sued NBC, claiming the network had violated its free speech rights. Mötley Crüe, of course, has no right to speak their trash on a network they don't own.
- Author Ed Klein whined that he was being "censored" when broadcast networks didn't invite him on to discuss his anti–Hillary Clinton book. This would only matter if the government were restricting Klein's access. It's not censorship of Klein when private media outlets using their own discretion just don't want to invest airtime in Klein's book.
- Actor Mickey Rooney filed a complaint with the FCC when Fox television declined to air a commercial for the Airborne cold remedy during the Super Bowl broadcast. That commercial featured a brief scene showing the aging actor's naked backside. Rooney asked the FCC to order Fox to air the commercial because "the public deserves to see it." The FCC ignored the request.
- School newspapers at high schools and even colleges don't provide students with full First Amendment protections. Courts have ruled that newspapers that are part of a school curriculum, supervised by school employees, and funded even in part by school money are subject to oversight by school administrators. In a sense, the administration is the owner of the school paper. Students wanting full free press rights should independently publish their own papers off of school property and with their own funds. They don't necessarily have a right to publish freely in a paper owned and managed by a school. By the way, school administrators should use this power with discretion. It really is important for students to learn about promoting the flow of ideas in an atmosphere that promotes the principles and responsibility of a free press.

- Four high-profile media organizations like the National Association of Broadcasters and the Radio-Television News Directors Association (RTNDA) threw collective fits when the National Football League (NFL) decided to restrict local television stations from shooting video on the sidelines of games. The organizations' protest letters to the NFL said the decision smacked of censorship and had First Amendment implications. The RTNDA president even said the NFL was "subverting the American tradition of a free press." Of course, this whining is all baseless. The NFL, as a private corporation, can regulate press access as it wishes. The sideline ban is consistent with rules of other professional sports organizations, the NCAA Final Four, and the Olympics, not to mention that the NFL provided video free of charge to the local stations of every play from every game. That didn't keep those professional associations from falsely claiming "rights" to have television videographers where the NFL didn't want them.

## No Forced Communication

- The *Baltimore Sun* newspaper went to court against Maryland governor Robert Ehrlich after he ordered that members of his executive staff could not talk with two particular *Sun* reporters. Ehrlich believed the reporters were unfair in their coverage. The newspaper said the two reporters had been denied their right to "speak and listen freely." While Ehrlich's ban was indeed antagonistic to the press, the *Sun* was misguided in its assertion that reporters have a right to speak to people who don't want to talk with them. The media have lost similar rulings in Cleveland and Youngstown, Ohio, with one federal judge saying people have a First Amendment right to *not* speak with reporters they don't appreciate.
- Each election cycle, various campaign reform groups push proposals to force television broadcasters to give unedited and free airtime to presidential candidates. This idea was even endorsed by former president Bill Clinton in his 1998 State of the Union address. Broadcasters already give candidates "free time" in news coverage and public affairs shows. This proposal, if ever forced on broadcasters, would likely be found unconstitutional in that it

would be forcing government messages into newsrooms where free press discretion is supposed to be used.

- A University of Utah student filed suit against the university after instructors in her acting class ordered her to act out roles that included foul language. She refused on religious grounds. A federal appeals court sided with the student and ordered the lower court to reconsider its initial ruling favoring the university. The student agreed to drop her suit after the university caved in, agreeing to implement a religious accommodation policy, pay the student's legal fees, and readmit her to the university.

## Deal with the Consequences

- The *New York Times* got all defensive when it absorbed multiple public scoldings after printing a controversial article about the government's surveillance program of international terrorist banking records. Executive editor Bill Keller got on his free press high horse and explained, "Our job . . . is to publish information" and that the publication of the bank surveillance served the "public interest." Other defenders of the *Times* dragged out the old argument about the public's "right to know." The First Amendment makes no demands on the press "to publish information," and newspapers only publish what they want to print, discarding countless other stories each day. The Constitution, by the way, says nothing about a "right to know" anything, and press advocates should stop asserting a right that's not there. The *Times* chose to run the story. Opponents chose to criticize that decision.
- Entertainer Whoopi Goldberg lost her job as a Slim-Fast spokesperson in 2004 after making off-color jokes during a political fund-raiser. She whined, "America's heart and soul is freedom of expression without fear of reprisal." She might have a point in terms of fear of reprisal from the government, but not in terms of image-conscious private companies that don't want sales impacted by an association with foul-mouthed political humorists.
- Singer Linda Ronstadt lost her Las Vegas singing gig for doing political commentary on stage. Filmmaker Michael Moore stood up for Ronstadt, saying she had a right to speak her mind. That's true in a public venue, but not in a private setting in which the owner

is paying her to sing and not for her political outbursts. The First Amendment doesn't protect a speaker from the repercussions of his speech.

- A Florida driver tried to run down U.S. congresswoman Katherine Harris with his car, saying he was exercising his "political expression." He was arrested anyway. There is a difference between expression and dangerous action.

- A community college instructor in Michigan was fired after using profanity in the classroom and then distributing copies of a student complaint letter, all in violation of the college's directives that he not do so. The instructor said the college violated his freedom of speech. A federal appeals court ruled that the behavior was not protected speech and that the college's directives were legitimate.

- A switchboard operator at CNN was fired when a viewer called to complain that the network had placed a large, black X over the face of Vice President Dick Cheney during a 2005 speech. The operator claimed the X was to make a point and was freedom of speech. CNN said an electronic malfunction has caused the X and fired the operator for inappropriately expressing personal views to the caller.

- A federal appeals court in 2003 upheld the firing of a mechanic who displayed Confederate flag stickers on his toolbox. He was fired for what the company said was a violation of their policy against harassment. The worker said the firing violated his First Amendment rights. The court sided with the employer saying that a private workplace is not constitutionally protected as a place for political expression.

- The Dixie Chicks country band became free-expression martyrs in 2003 after a number of radio stations stopped playing the Chicks' songs. The radio stations were reacting to the public criticisms of President Bush made by lead singer Natalie Maines. Fellow entertainer Elton John stood up for the Chicks, saying they had the right to say whatever they wanted. That's certainly true, but the radio stations have every right to express themselves by not playing artists they don't support. The Chicks' pity party continued in 2006 when both NBC and the CW network refused to air commercials promoting the Chicks's movie, *Shut Up and Sing*, because the networks felt the ads were disparaging to President Bush. The movie's producer, Harvey Weinstein, said these "courageous entertainers" were being "blacklisted for exercising their right of free speech." The television networks, of course, have no obligation to provide the Chicks with a forum to exercise their free speech.

- A San Diego police officer was fired for posting indecent video of himself on the Internet. He filed suit saying his off-duty free speech was protected. The Supreme Court upheld the firing saying such "speech" was damaging to the mission of the employer.

## My Speech Is Okay. Yours Is Not.
- When Congress passed a law denying federal funds to colleges that didn't allow military recruiters on campus, professors at dozens of law schools sued the government, claiming that the forced appearance of military recruiters damaged the freedom of expression of the professors. The Supreme Court ruled in favor of the military recruiters, saying that recruiters' presence didn't affect the ability of the professors to speak out against the military as they saw fit.

- Shock radio personality Howard Stern moved from over-the-air broadcasting to satellite to avoid oversight by the FCC, which currently regulates terrestrial radio but not satellite radio broadcasts. Stern said the move was, in part, to protect his free speech rights. Later, in a published interview, Stern talked about a gag order he had placed on radio competitors Opie and Anthony when all of them were working at Infinity Broadcasting. Stern said he believed in censoring people he considered his enemies: "I believe in censorship when it benefits me."

- Colleges are proud to give cover to far-out speakers and professors, excusing their harsh rhetoric as academic freedom. That is, until speakers show up with messages that don't support accepted campus ideologies. In recent years, conservative commentators Ann Coulter, William Kristol, and David Horowitz had pies thrown at them during campus speeches. Salad dressing was dumped on Pat Buchanan.

- Some students at Columbia University forced a premature ending of a presentation by two members of the Minutemen, the independent group that patrols the border between the United States and Mexico. Minutemen founder Jim Gilchrist and member Marvin Stewart were forced from the stage when rowdy students took over the stage and upended furniture.

- DePaul University in Chicago invited controversial University of Colorado professor Ward Churchill to speak on campus, but then banned a student group from posting flyers protesting Churchill's appearance. The university later relented. As a private university, the administration can pretty much ban whatever it wants, but the oppression of dissent on public issues runs contrary to the supposed value of academic freedom.

- Lawmakers in the state of Washington passed a law that prohibited political candidates from lying about opponents. Defining what constituted a political lie was bound to be a problem. An appeals court, appropriately, struck down the law and let opposing politicians fend for themselves, as they have for more than two hundred years.

- Private citizen Harvey Kash was arrested outside a New York courthouse for telling lawyer jokes. Some lawyers apparently didn't like Kash's sense of humor. Thankfully, a grand jury threw out the charge of disorderly conduct.

- The San Francisco Board of Supervisors passed a ban in 2005 against any spoken comment at city meetings that could be deemed insensitive based on personal characteristics like height, weight, or place of birth. Board president Aaron Peskin said the ban was not an attack on free speech. Oh really?

- Antiwar groups complained to the Clear Channel media corporation about the U.S. Navy being a sponsor for a summer concert series promoted by Clear Channel radio station KMEL in San Francisco. The protestors wanted the Navy messages removed and threatened to challenge KMEL's FCC license.

- Radio personality Mancow Muller filed suit against a listener because that listener filed multiple complaints with the FCC about the content of Mancow's broadcasts. Mancow, who had been fined on several occasions by the FCC for broadcasting indecent content, said he sued the complaining listener in order to get his free speech rights restored. A federal judge refused to hear the suit. Voices of opposition have their free speech rights, too.

- Journalists want the privilege of not having to disclose confidential sources, even when ordered by a court to do so. They say that allows them to more fully disclose government misbehavior by encouraging confidential sources to come forward. They've managed to get "shield laws" passed in over thirty states to protect themselves from such court orders. Journalism organizations are pressing Congress for shield protection from federal courts. This "press exceptionalism" asserts rights for journalists that average citizens don't have. Nothing in the constitutional guarantee of free press provides for such special treatment. Although court decisions have consistently held that journalists can be required to reveal their sources when legal circumstances dictate, the press still works to create legislation that would give them the same status for private confidences that lawyers, medical doctors, and clergy have. But journalists aren't the same as professionals like doctors and lawyers. Journalists have no formal certification or educational standards. The information they gather is designed for public dissemination, unlike the other professionals, who gather information from private people for private purposes.

Clearly, confusion reigns regarding the First Amendment, and the courts have a difficult job in sorting out the challenging issues involved. The challenge in finding the proper perspective on free expression in our nation is complicated by the many citizens and media organizations that have insufficient understanding or appreciation for what the First Amendment means and doesn't mean. Heavy metal band Metallica has performed a song titled "Free Speech for the Dumb." While it is the American way that everybody gets to work his mouth, a better understanding of free expression rights and more careful consideration of our messages would go a long way in making a more civil and enlightened society, making our free speech less dumb.

# CHAPTER THREE

༒

# Sex, Skin, and Swearing

A major front in the culture wars is being fought on America's broadcast airwaves. Network television and radio programmers, falsely wrapping themselves in the First Amendment, have infiltrated publicly owned broadcast channels with increasing amounts of profanity, sexual language, and skin. For years, the public sat back and took it. The public's government appointed watchdog, the Federal Communications Commission (FCC), casually sidestepped its congressionally mandated duty, largely ignoring the elephant in the living room and taking a laissez-faire approach to regulating indecent broadcast content. Meanwhile, network executives in Hollywood and New York took advantage of the circumstances to push back cultural standards, creating edgier and edgier programs. The content war on America's airwaves was being won by those whose values hardly meshed with those of the public, or adhered to federal regulations.

At last, a cultural counterattack began in December 2003. A Senate resolution, offered by Alabama senator Jeff Sessions, blasted the FCC for its lax enforcement of broadcast indecency standards. It passed unanimously. Sessions's resolution came in response to an FCC Enforcement Bureau decision that the use of a particular F-word by rock singer Bono during a live Golden Globe Awards show did not violate on-air content standards. Bono, while on the awards stand during a live

NBC network broadcast, uttered the phrase, "This is really ****ing brilliant." The FCC's commissioners overruled the Enforcement Bureau's mistake in early 2004, but still failed to assess a financial penalty on NBC. The egregiousness of the initial ruling, coupled with the wet noodle punishment by the full commission, served to get Congress into the act.

The Bono incident was the match that ignited congressional and public mobilization against indecent broadcast content, but the issue came to full flame after the infamous 2004 Super Bowl halftime show. It is one thing to have seedy content in stupid sitcoms, music videos, or prime-time dramas, but when the values of the showbiz world crashed into the most Americanized of television events, the Super Bowl, the public outcry was immediate and loud. Once performer Justin Timberlake removed part of singer Janet Jackson's costume during the now unforgettable "wardrobe malfunction," the FCC could no longer ignore the obvious—that network TV was not bashful about pushing the indecency envelope and that the public was fed up.

The debate regarding indecent content on broadcast airwaves has raged ever since Super Bowl 2004. The FCC has used this time to try to get its enforcement act together. Broadcasters have talked about restraint, but have mostly complained about their contrived free speech rights while continuing to test just how distasteful and profane they can make their content and still avoid FCC fines. Congress postured for two years about getting tough with broadcasters before finally passing legislation in 2006 to increase broadcaster indecency penalties tenfold. Each broadcast incident deemed indecent by the FCC can now get a broadcaster fined up to $325,000. Congress has contemplated extending indecency regulation to cable and satellite broadcasting but has not yet moved in that direction. Meanwhile, broadcasters gripe about being held accountable and are taking their FCC challenges to court. Clearly, the cultural war over broadcast indecency has many battles to come.

## Key Historical Perspectives Needed to Understand Indecency Regulation

The foundation for government regulation of broadcasting was established in the 1920s during a series of conferences called by Secretary of

Commerce Herbert Hoover. The oversight of the blossoming radio industry was dumped into Hoover's lap, and he quickly discovered that a federal regulatory structure would be needed to guide and manage broadcasting. At the time, the radio industry was highly disorganized, with broadcasters intentionally interfering with one another's signals and claiming certain frequencies as their private domains. Hoover's conferences called leading engineers, educators, and civic leaders together to discuss how to best oversee broadcasting. The key philosophic direction that Hoover established as a result of the meetings was that broadcast airwaves belonged to the public, not to the broadcasters who happened to be using the frequency at any given time. That philosophic underpinning was legislated in the Radio Act of 1927 and later the Communications Act of 1934, and still holds true today. Given that the airwaves belong to the public, a federal agency—the FCC— was established to see that the public's interests were maintained even while commercial broadcasters used the frequencies as temporary franchise holders. In a sense, publicly owned broadcast airwaves are like publicly owned highways or parks, with government oversight to make sure the users of those public resources, indeed, keep the public welfare served.

Congress determined that broadcasters must serve the "public interest, convenience, and necessity," and gave the FCC discretionary regulatory power in determining who should have broadcast licenses and whether those licensees were, indeed, serving the public interest. Congress legislated its prohibition against obscene, indecent, and profane content in the United States Code, Section 1464 of title 18, thus establishing its intent as law. Thus, the regulatory framework for broadcasting was established, and despite court challenges over the years, the FCC's power to regulate the industry and to define the public interest standard has been maintained.

With the cultural turmoil of the late 1960s and early 1970s came the urge by broadcasters to push the content tolerance of the FCC. Radio programs, in particular, began to test which topics and words could be broadcast without FCC penalty. In October 1973, WBAI-FM, a community station in New York City owned by Pacifica Foundation, broadcast a program that would lead to a Supreme Court ruling establishing the rules of indecency enforcement up to and including this current era.

WBAI-FM was presenting an afternoon broadcast that dealt generally with the attitudes people have toward language and certain expression. As part of that broadcast, the station aired a recorded comedy monologue by George Carlin called "Filthy Words." In the monologue, Carlin listed and discussed the seven words that weren't allowed on public airwaves. In advance of the Carlin recording, WBAI-FM had issued an on-air warning that the content to follow could be offensive to some listeners. A couple of weeks later, a man wrote to the FCC to complain about the broadcast, saying that he had heard the program while driving in his car with his teenage son. Although this was the only complaint received, the FCC reviewed the case and issued a warning letter to be placed in the WBAI-FM files.

Pacifica Foundation appealed the FCC sanction through the courts, with the case winding up before the Supreme Court in 1978. In a narrow 5–4 decision, the court backed the FCC and defended the commission's role in regulating indecent content on broadcast airwaves. The court backed the FCC's operational definition of indecency as "language that describes, in terms patently offensive as measured by contemporary community standards for the broadcast medium, sexual or excretory activities and organs." The court affirmed that this was an appropriate case in which the FCC should exercise its power, and that keeping indecent broadcast content from children was a legitimate interest of the government. The focus on protecting children led to implementation of the FCC's "safe harbor" standard that restricts broadcast of questionable content between 6 a.m. and 10 p.m., times in which there is a reasonable expectation that children could be in the audience. The court rejected Pacifica's concern that government regulation of indecent content would lead to self-censorship by broadcasters, and said that even if broadcasters' self-restriction kept some otherwise free speech expressions off the air, "they surely lie at the periphery of First Amendment concern." The court said that the "uniquely pervasive presence" of broadcasting in the lives of Americans provided the government opportunity to regulate those communications in ways that would not be allowed constitutionally for other methods of communication. One justice compared indecent broadcast messages to "a pig in the parlor," indicating that regulatory power is appropriate when the pig leaves the barnyard. In short, the Supreme Court confirmed that broadcasters have no constitutionally protected "right" to broadcast indecent material.

## Media Whining and Complaining

It seems simple enough that with the relevant law and court decisions in effect, broadcasters would understand that neither the First Amendment nor Congress will protect indecent content on the public's broadcast airwaves. Instead, like spoiled kids who don't want their discipline, broadcasters have constantly whined and griped about their free speech rights to talk dirty on the air, about how the FCC's rules are too confusing and hard to follow, and how they are just giving the public what it wants.

Media industry leaders have offered a steady barrage of self-pitying complaints and bogus arguments in recent years, trying to convince regulators and the public of how oppressed they are for having to take decency and public taste into programming consideration. A prime example of such misdirection came in 2005 when National Association of Broadcasters chairman Philip Lombardo addressed the Media Institute. Lombardo, the CEO of the Citadel Communications broadcasting corporation, said that broadcasters are "the best arbiters of program choices" and that they could make decisions on their own without government oversight. He said the broadcast industry suffered from "unprecedented anxiety" because of the FCC's renewed interest in indecency enforcement. In a remarkable "sky is falling" assertion, Lombardo said it was the "viewers and listeners who suffer the most from the government crackdown" and questioned whether broadcasters would have to "dumb down" content to avoid FCC sanctions. Thus, by this Lombardo logic, it is the edgy content that is intellectually sophisticated and that programs without such material are for the less brainy audience members. Lombardo went on to complain that many content complaints to the FCC come from activist groups and/or people who might not have even seen the programs they are complaining about. So, while pushing for absolute free expression rights for broadcasters to program whatever they see fit on publicly owned airwaves, Lombardo asserts that activist groups should stifle themselves from exercising their right to complain about those programs. Further, why must a citizen expose himself to indecent content to qualify to protest it? Most people have never witnessed a murder but still don't approve of it. Lombardo even threatened that broadcasters having to pay FCC fines for indecency would no longer be able to afford to broadcast news or public affairs programs that serve the community. And so goes the kindergarten logic of the broadcast industry.

The Media Institute gave CBS chairman Sumner Redstone a platform to pound his chest about indecency regulation when the institute gave Redstone its Freedom of Speech Award in 2006. Redstone's free-speech accomplishment was to file court appeals against the FCC because the FCC had the audacity to fine CBS for indecency violations. The Media Institute, which bills itself as a "research foundation specializing in communications policy," is funded by the nation's biggest media corporations and is overseen by top executives from those media giants. Its obvious purpose is to protect the interests of those media corporations. Redstone told the Media Institute's believers that the media industry was "living with a great deal of fear" because of increased government content scrutiny. He warned that government fines could reduce creativity in the artistic community, somehow believing that creativity is linked to indecent content, and that the only outlet for indecent content is on broadcast airwaves.

An editorial in the trade magazine *Broadcasting & Cable* (*B&C*) encouraged broadcasters with the headline "Fight the Tyranny of the Minority." The editorial dismissed a flood of indecency complaints to the FCC as not being "a barometer of broad-based opposition to media content." Thus, according to the editorial, mass protests from members of the Parents Television Council are irrelevant. The editorial also moaned that one citizen complainant, along with three of the five FCC commissioners, could get a broadcaster fined. Thus, as the editorial pointed out, four people could make a decision as to "what millions in the rest of the country can see and hear." That might well be true, but the broadcasting magazine seems less worried that three or four guys around a network table in Hollywood are constantly making decisions about what millions of people will see. Indeed, Howard Stern, the shock radio deejay, by himself decides each day what millions of people hear. Broadcasters have refused to accept that it is the content of shows that is evaluated when the FCC determines sanctions, not the scorecard of how many people have complained. This point was made clear by former FCC chairman Michael Powell in an op-ed in late 2004: "Under the law, we must independently evaluate whether a program violates the standard, no matter whether the program in question generates a single complaint or thousands."

Other editorials in *B&C* in recent months have labeled FCC indecency enforcement "indefensible" and "a joke." *B&C* overlooked the fact that the FCC is mandated to be in the indecency enforcement business, writing, "The FCC commissioners should feel uncomfortable making content decisions. We hope they feel so uncomfortable they avoid any rulings." This is like suggesting that the police stop making drug busts or making murder arrests because it might not be pleasant.

Others in the media industry are just as predictable and consistent in their whining about indecent content regulation. Once the FCC sabers started rattling after the Super Bowl fiasco, television director and producer R. J. Cutler said the FCC was waging "an assault on the First Amendment." He went on to say, "It's certainly a dark day. When you prohibit freedom of speech in any area of American life, it is a slippery, slippery slope." Thus, all speech is equally valuable in this absolutist reasoning. Public Broadcasting Service president Pat Mitchell expressed concern about FCC indecency regulations, saying, "They're not as clear as all of us in the media business would like them to be."

A batch of FCC rulings in early 2006 on television content complaints sparked yet another round of fearmongering by broadcasters. Famed television producer Steven Bochco, in an interview, called the FCC rulings "blank-blank chilling. . . . You just can't say anything or do anything or show anything or tell a controversial story." Oh sure, all controversial stories must have indecent content. The executive producer of *Family Guy* said the "rules don't seem logical or consistent." Tom Fontana, the creator and producer of WB's show *The Bedford Diaries*, a zany look at the exciting world of college students taking a class on human sexuality, said he "found the ruling incomprehensible." *B&C* returned to its shrill rhetoric, claiming the FCC rulings were "confusing" and would lead to "self-censorship." Self-control would be another way of looking at this matter. If a broadcast producer can't keep from programming indecent content, then the FCC must step in to provide the enforcement sanctions.

Timothy Busfield, the co–executive producer of CBS's *Without a Trace*, one of the programs sanctioned by the FCC's 2006 rulings, said the FCC was diminishing broadcast television's authenticity. In an interview, Busfield said, "It's frustrating that people on network TV cannot speak the way people actually speak today. . . . We have to speak their speak . . . or it becomes impossible for the audience to take the journey with us." Well, who knows what journey is being discussed here? Maybe a journey into a cultural cesspool. The argument, however, that network programs have to have indecent or profane language to reach audiences has no merit on several levels. First, nobody really thinks that fictional prime-time television is authentic in the first place. Audiences watching thoroughly unreal and contrived dramas, sitcoms, and, yes, "reality" shows will hardly think the programs are authentic just because producers want to throw in some raunchy dialogue. Next, while it might well be true that coarse language seeps into the "way people actually speak today," people don't speak that way in all contexts. Even the most lowbrow of speakers has the gumption to not use foul language in business settings, in educational settings, in government settings, and in any setting for which proper decorum is expected. Broadcast television, being firmly placed in the public sphere, using public airwaves, and being disseminated to the broadest of audiences, surely deserves a basic level of politeness, regardless of how Busfield and his pals speak in real life at their collective frat house. There are countless examples of powerful and authentic television programs over the years that avoided offensive language and images and still told dramatic or comedic stories of note.

When the FCC began to review tapes of sports broadcasts for vulgar remarks cut loose during live sports events, broadcast executives predictably started fussing. In a published report, one anonymous broadcast executive accused the FCC of seeking to end live broadcast television. Of course, that is not the FCC's goal, but you wouldn't know it if you just listened to the media's Chicken Littles. All broadcasters need to do in order to broadcast live events, including sports, is use the available technology that delays a broadcast signal long enough for a producer to bleep out any foul language that might erupt from an athlete or fan. That equipment, while expensive, is cheaper than paying fines and cheaper than most of the high-tech replay and slow-motion gizmos that broadcasters have already invested in. Beyond that, broadcasters could use their heads and not do live sports interviews with angry coaches and rambunctious fans. Crowd microphones can be placed in less risky places than the front of the frat section of a college basketball game. A seven-second delay of a live sports event is not going to disrupt the spontaneity of the game, but can stop the public airing of expletives that sometimes emerge at such events.

The producers of indecent entertainment programming have ready allies on the journalism side of the media world. Apparently incapable of distinguishing between the context of news and entertainment, Radio-Television News Directors Association (RTNDA) chairman Dan Shelley responded to the FCC's renewed interest in indecency enforcement by calling the crackdown "draconian," saying it would have a "chilling effect on live news coverage." An RTNDA news release said the FCC was unconstitutionally limiting "the ability of broadcast journalists to provide accurate and insightful reporting to the public." Sandra Baron of the Media Law Resource Center wailed that the FCC's action could "only result in less coverage of matters of public concern." Never mind that the FCC has only once ever fined a station for indecent content in a news program. That "news" segment in 2002 on San Francisco's KRON featured a segment during a morning news show in which performers were interviewed from the stage show "Puppetry of the Penis." One of the performers exposed himself while demonstrating "genital origami." This is hardly the kind of news content the RTNDA and Media Law Resource Center should be wasting their collective free speech–protection breath on. Clearly, this broadcast segment was not a matter of public concern and provided no insightful reporting for the public. The shrill warnings from journalists regarding indecency enforcement completely overlook the fact that the FCC has bent over backward to exempt news programs from indecency fines. The FCC chose not to fine CBS's The Early Show even though a particular b-s word was uttered by a Survivor contestant during a shameless CBS "news" interview to promote its primetime reality show. The FCC said the word was not considered indecent or profane because it had occurred during a news program. Of course, the segment in question was clearly more promotion-oriented than news-oriented, but the FCC is trying to give journalistic content some benefit of the doubt.

Conservative talk radio host Rush Limbaugh added to the alarmism after Clear Channel Communications dropped Howard Stern's show from Clear Channel–owned radio stations. Ignoring the fact that it was Clear Channel's decision to drop Stern, and not the FCC's, Limbaugh said, "When the federal government gets involved in this, I get a little frightened." He asserted that people should not sit by and let the government make decisions to "censor" content, adding, "I am in the free speech business." Here again, a false fear is raised that legislated government restriction on indecent content somehow threatens political or news discussion that would clearly be constitutionally protected.

Former FCC chairman Reed Hundt, who oversaw the FCC during the first four years of the Clinton administration, gave a speech to the Duke University School of Law in spring 2005. He wailed that the FCC's post–Super Bowl indecency initiatives were the biggest threat to the First Amendment since the McCarthy era. Continuing to frighten the audience with false comparisons, Hundt asserted that the FCC's indecency enforcement against episodes like the Jackson-Timberlake fiasco could stifle television news coverage of the war in Iraq! Television journalists, he suggested, might be hesitant to broadcast real footage from the war zone for fear of FCC penalties if that material contained questionable language. This clearly ineffective argument overlooks two key factors. First, the news context of such a war report would keep the FCC from seeking action, if such material were, indeed, broadcast. Second, is it even essential that actual foul language be included in a war report in order to enhance the public's understanding of the story? Surely the public can be made fully aware of the harsh complexities of the war, and its political implications, while bleeping out foul language from the war zone.

As previously mentioned, one precaution against bad language or other unexpected content that comes when broadcasters do live broadcasts is the installation of delaying technology. Not surprisingly, however, broadcast managers have moaned about the costliness of this solution, even though they think nothing of spending hundreds of thousands of dollars on jet copters, fancy sets, consultants, and expensive talent. Typical of the resistance is this trade magazine comment from a San Diego television news director: "It [delaying technology for live broadcasts] runs counter to the whole definition of news. We want it to be up to the minute, live and not distort what people are seeing in any way." Of course, news producers routinely distort content with sensationalism and selective coverage, not to mention that a delay of several seconds would have a negligible effect on audience perception.

When President George W. Bush signed legislation in the summer of 2006 that raised potential indecency fines to $325,000 per incident, Fox entertainment network president Peter Liguori complained that "none of the [networks'] business plans are designed to handle such huge fines." Of course, network resources are quite ample and capable of paying such fines if needed, but the better business plan in light of the new fine structure would be to avoid indecent content in the first place.

## Media Shirking Responsibility and Pushing Unworkable Solutions

Media executives are unwilling to take responsibility for programming indecent content and intend to keep airing it, all the while reassuring the public that this is a good thing because they are standing up for free speech and the First Amendment. In a warped bit of reasoning, having sufficient indecent content on publicly owned airwaves is supposed to be a good thing for the First Amendment. Although it is relatively few shows and stations that actually have problems with indecent content issues, virtually all broadcasters and media producers want to stand up for those who do engage in airing such material. In 2004, a grab bag of broadcasters, artist groups, and media corporations filed protests to the FCC, warning that indecency policies were chilling free speech in broadcasting. No mention was made of which essential content was now left out of the national dialogue. CBS chairman Les Moonves reacted to FCC action on the wardrobe malfunction by saying the government was infringing on free speech. The TV Watch coalition, made up of various broadcast corporations and networks, formed in 2005 to fight government control of broadcast content. Actor Joe Pantoliano, copresident of the Creative Coalition and part of the TV Watch effort, said their cause was to preserve "the very basic freedoms that the First Amendment provides for our children and their children." TV Watch member Adam Thierer supports the "anything goes" of media regulation, saying, "In a free society, different people will have different values and tolerance levels when it comes to speech" and that "discretion over content should be housed in private, not public, hands." He said the cause of TV Watch was to "protect the First Amendment and our heritage of freedom of speech." Who knew that the principle of free expression in our society hinges on whether broadcasters can talk dirty and show skin on the airwaves?

To keep the heat off their social irresponsibility, media executives have taken to pushing the burden of maintaining societal standards for taste onto everybody and anybody else. In a 2001 speech to the National Association of Broadcasters, MPAA (Motion Picture Association of America) president Jack Valenti acknowledged that incivility was "invading the culture of the community" but failed to mention the role the media play in pushing that cultural decline. He said it was just par for the course that the media would "produce both the tawdry and the superior," but anybody wanting the media cleaned up was against free speech. Absolving the media from any social obligation, Valenti said, "Schools, churches and parents must instill values that protect themselves from objectionable material."

The government, with society's broad support, has instituted countless regulations to protect children. It's against the law to sell cigarettes or alcohol to kids. Kids in cars must be protected by car seats. Kids aren't allowed in casinos. There are federal laws that restrict the amount of commercials that can be aired during broadcast programs targeted to kids. But when it comes to protecting kids from indecent broadcast content, the media industry dumps sole responsibility onto the shoulders of parents. This sounds like a good idea, but it is no more workable than having parents be solely responsible for keeping their kids from smoking, truancy, or the many other things kids can do wrong and for which society takes on a shared responsibility. Not to mention, of course, that many kids watch television or listen to radio when parents aren't around, or that some kids might watch inappropriate material with the parents' approval.

National public service campaigns by broadcasters have tried to promote the use of V-chips and on-air ratings warnings as ways to protect kids from offensive material. The National Cable and Telecommunications Association has orchestrated a series of public service announcements telling parents to "Take Control. It's Easy." The campaign urges parents to pay more attention to the on-screen rating icons and to use the V-chip blocking devices in their television sets. A separate campaign, with the same sense of dumping responsibility, was launched in 2005 by a group of media outfits, including NBC, Viacom, Fox, Comcast, and Time Warner. The campaign, called "Pause Parent Play," focused on having parents pay more attention to what their kids watch and to use the blocking tools available to shield kids from inappropriate content.

There are multiple problems with the "solutions" being forwarded by these self-interested campaigns. First, philosophically, the media refuse to absorb any responsibility for the content they create. Second, the focus is on protecting kids, and no consideration is made of protecting society as a whole from the culture of sleaze.

The practical problems are also noteworthy. V-chips are programmable devices installed in televisions that allow for the blocking of inappropriate content. The Telecommunications Act of 1996 has required all television sets manufactured since the beginning of 2000 to have these devices. From an engineering standpoint, these sound great. From a parental use standpoint, the V-chip has been a bust. As of 2005, only 15 percent of parents had ever used the V-chip to block programs. Most others never knew V-chips existed or how to operate them. In addition, V-chips won't block programs that are not labeled correctly. The Parents Television Council reports that many programs are not labeled correctly and that the networks are inconsistent in their labeling practices. Further, V-chips can't stop live programs in progress. For example, even operational V-chips would not have stopped the 2004 Super Bowl halftime show and the Bono Golden Globes outburst.

As for the ratings icons that appear on the screen at the start of programs, most viewers don't notice them. Research indicates that most viewers don't know what the little letters stand for anyway. Who would know that D stands for suggestive dialogue or that FV stands for fantasy violence?

The worst failing, however, of these self-serving campaigns that make parents solely responsible for kids' viewing is that there is no help for those millions of kids whose parents don't "Take Control" or use "Pause Parent Play."

## Government Inaction Sent the Wrong Message

One legitimate point made by the media industry in its protest against indecency enforcement is that the FCC has been inconsistent over the years in its concern for the problem. This outlook emerged most noticeably in the 1980s during the Reagan era's effort to deregulate government. Reagan FCC chairman Mark Fowler took this philosophy to heart and worked to get the FCC out of content issues. He denied that broadcasters had any responsibility to the public and, instead, urged the FCC to treat broadcasters merely as businesses for which the FCC would serve as a traffic cop to make sure that engineering standards were in place, but nothing more. In the laissez-faire regulatory world, Fowler believed, "television is just another appliance. It's a toaster with pictures." The Clinton FCC was little better, with chairman Reed Hundt taking an absolutist view of broadcasters' free expression rights. Further confusing things, in the ten years 1993–2002, the FCC cancelled twelve fines it had earlier decided to assess. During the period of lax enforcement, the FCC dismissed hundreds of legitimate complaints, rationalizing that slang terms used on air to describe excretory functions or the male anatomy were just used to express anger and were not necessarily presented for shock value, as if either of these distinctions excused the content. In short, the FCC was buffaloed by lame broadcaster arguments about free speech and marketplace determination, and simply didn't want to engage in the fight. The congressional outrage and Super Bowl fiasco of 2004 finally got the FCC into indecency enforcement gear. In 2004, the FCC handed out more fines to broadcasters than had been issued in the previous thirteen years combined.

The inconsistent FCC enforcement record over the last twenty-plus years, however, cannot be allowed to become a rationale for weak enforcement practices now. The laws on the books and the guiding Supreme Court decision are the same as before the FCC lost its compass on broadcast standards. Selective enforcement of the law is as old as law itself. A police officer who stops you for speeding today will not be sympathetic to your argument that you drove the same speed on that road last week without being ticketed.

# Recent FCC Decisions Keep the Pressure On

The FCC handed down a barrage of indecency decisions in early 2006, giving notice that the battle was back on. The rulings were the first to come out under the leadership of new chairman Kevin Martin, who made it clear that a new sheriff was in town. CBS received fines of $550,000 for the Super Bowl "wardrobe malfunction," and another $3.5 million fine spread out among its CBS-owned and -affiliated stations for an episode of the prime-time show *Without a Trace* that depicted a teen sex party. The WB was fined for an episode of the program *The Surreal Life 2*, which showed scenes, pixilated as they were, from a porn star's pool party. Telemundo, a Los Angeles television station owned by NBC, was fined for showing a movie that contained a graphic rape scene. Other fines targeted television stations for various other offenses, including the broadcast of suggestive music videos and coarse language. The commission found four other television broadcasts between 2002 and 2004 to have violated indecency rules, but chose not to sanction the offending stations because of the FCC's own admission that its "precedent at the time of the broadcast did not clearly indicate that the Commission would take enforcement action." The commission also dismissed twenty-eight other indecency cases that included questionable language and innuendo, providing analysis as to why those broadcasts did not meet the standard for sanctions.

Not surprisingly, the FCC can't keep anybody happy. The television networks and other broadcast owners have ganged up to appeal the decisions in federal court, claiming the rulings are unconstitutional. The broadcasters might actually find a sympathetic court at the lower levels of the appeals process, but likely won't when the Supreme Court eventually gets the case in a couple of years. The interest groups wanting more forceful FCC action, like Morality in Media, also criticized the FCC for letting some cases slide. FCC member Michael Copps, a longtime proponent of tougher content sanctions, recognized the difficulty of keeping everybody happy. He issued a statement that said it is not possible to provide "100 percent certain guidance" regarding what the commission will find indecent. He acknowledged that the recent decisions "may not satisfy those who clamor for immediate certainty in an uncertain world."

National Association of Broadcasters (NAB) president David Rehr responded to the 2006 FCC fines by singing out of the same old song-book. He told the NAB convention that the organization had "no objection" to following indecency rules, but that the FCC rulings "did little to clarify these rules" and that they needed "clearer guidance from the FCC." Clarity is impossible, of course, for broadcasters who won't cooperate.

What's important here, however, is not that the FCC can't keep everybody happy. The important development in the 2006 decisions is that the FCC has finally taken back its designated role of enforcing federal broadcast indecency laws. The commission surely will make mistakes and confusing judgments at times along the way, but at least it is not simply ignoring its responsibility as it has so often for more than two decades.

## Where Indecency Enforcement Goes from Here

The future of federal indecency enforcement hinges largely on how the Supreme Court deals with the appeals to the FCC's 2006 decisions. In the intervening time, however, the struggle will continue in several arenas. As previously mentioned, legislation to increase indecency fines passed through Congress in June 2006 and was signed by President Bush. The new fine structure allows the FCC to penalize offending broadcasters $325,000 per violation, ten times the previous limit. This legislation was sorely needed to get the attention of those megamedia corporations for which the smaller fine is pocket change. As former FCC chairman Michael Powell said in a 2004 speech, the current fine levels were "peanuts," and "just a cost of doing business" for broadcasters who want to thumb their noses at the FCC and the public.

The "safe harbor" time frame might well need review in the near future. The Supreme Court decision to allow more edgy content on the broadcast media from 10 p.m. to 6 a.m. was made in 1978 with the assumption that children would not likely be in the audience at that time. Nearly thirty years later, much ratings data proves that plenty of kids are, indeed, watching television after 10 p.m.

Heated debate can be expected on whether the FCC should extend its indecency enforcement into the realm of cable and satellite broadcasting. Historically, the FCC has limited its enforcement to over-the-air broadcasts and avoided dealing with programming delivered to the home via subscription cable or satellite. Many activists, however, and some congressional leaders believe it is time to get the raunchy programs of cable and satellite into the net. Clearly, now that upwards of 85 percent of all viewers are receiving their programming via cable or satellite, the distinction between over-air broadcast and cable/satellite is totally worn out. The average viewer doesn't even know the difference between over-the-air and cable content—it's all just television to him. The prevailing rationale that indecency enforcement is needed to protect children is just as relevant for kids watching cable as it is for kids watching programs delivered over the air. Further, the fact that cable and satellite programs are delivered via utility poles and/or frequency channels overseen by government regulators should get this content into the discussion. In an odd bit of logic, many over-air broadcasters, who don't like the idea of FCC enforcement generally, would actually like indecency enforcement directed at cable and satellite, believing that it would level the playing field for trying to reach the media consumers who want the edgier fare. Some people argue that the FCC has no business regulating channels to which consumers willingly subscribe and invite into their homes. They should consider, however, that the FCC already regulates cable/satellite content for commercialization in children's programming, with regard to political advertising rules, and for sponsorship identification rules, so that foot is already in the door. A possible hint that the FCC might have an eye toward cable and satellite can be found in the "Frequently Asked Questions" section of the FCC website. The answer to a question about whether the FCC's rules apply to cable and satellite programming begins with the phrase, "In the past . . ." The implication, of course, is that things could be different in the future.

A current legal barrier to extending indecency regulation to cable and satellite is a Supreme Court decision in 2000 that gave a victory to cable systems. The Court said the Communications Decency Act passed by Congress in 1996 was too restrictive in that it required cable operators to scramble adult-channel content or carry such content between 10 p.m. and 6 a.m. The Court's 5–4 majority opinion, written by Justice Anthony Kennedy, said giving subscribers the opportunity to obtain blocking devices was sufficient and provided a "less restrictive alternative" than banning the material altogether. Those less restrictive alternatives, while technically viable, are, in a practical sense, not effectively shielding children when parents don't have them installed and operational. In his dissent, Justice Stephen Breyer indicated the majority had not made "a realistic assessment." Justice Clarence Thomas surprisingly sided with the majority in this case, breaking ranks with his usual ally, conservative Justice Antonin Scalia. Should a future such case arrive at the Supreme Court, any change of heart by Justice Thomas could well change the Court's direction on such cable content matters.

One avenue being advocated by FCC chairman Kevin Martin and some prominent congressmen is for cable companies to provide what is being referred to as "a la carte" programming. Under this setup, subscribers would consciously choose the cable channels they want delivered into their homes, thus actively avoiding channels carrying questionable content. Cable companies don't like the idea partly because of the logistical challenges, but mostly because of the revenue they would likely lose. Cable distributors make money for every channel they distribute. Consumers closing off a bunch of channels would hit the cable companies in the pocketbook. This plan, however, seems like a great compromise in dealing with cable content. It empowers consumers and diminishes the prospect of further regulation. If cable companies stall on this proposal, Congress might well legislate some form of an a la carte requirement, and then the legal battles would surely begin.

A case in Michigan bears notice in the arena of cable content and could be a sign of future directions. A Michigan state appeals court decision in May 2005, which was not taken up by the Michigan Supreme Court, ruled that nudity distributed on cable television is not protected speech and that Michigan's indecent exposure law includes television. In fact, the appeals court said that television nudity could be more powerful than other public exposure and that the government's interest in public morality was more important than the defendant's free expression rights. Although this case has no application beyond the state of Michigan, the strategy of fighting cable content through the indecent exposure statutes could be adopted in other jurisdictions.

# Citizen Empowerment to Take On Offensive Content

Public opinion polls in recent years have consistently shown the citizenry wants stricter government enforcement of indecency regulations. A poll conducted in March 2005 by the Pew Research Center for the People and the Press showed 75 percent of respondents wanted tighter enforcement of government rules on television content during times when kids could be watching. A large majority, 69 percent, favored the higher fines proposed in Congress, and 60 percent want cable television included in indecency standards. Another 2005 poll, conducted by Harris Interactive for the Morality in Media organization, found that 53 percent of the respondents felt the government was doing a poor job of "maintaining community standards of decency on broadcast TV." Other polls show similar results.

Given these results, one must wonder why more citizens don't follow up on their concerns with protests to the FCC and/or the broadcasters that originate the questionable programs. Several reasons could be suggested. First, many viewers likely do just change the channel to something less offensive, buying into the broadcast industry argument to just not watch what you don't like. While there is some simple logic to this notion, it is like telling motorists to just get off of dangerous highways that are not patrolled sufficiently by the police. Just like motorists who should have the opportunity to travel any public highway safely, television viewers should know that their publicly owned channels are safe in a content sense, even if they aren't watching at any particular time. Next, many viewers likely believe their complaints would have no impact. But as we know from the Supreme Court's Pacifica ruling that remains in place today, a single complaint can lead to a landmark decision. Further, the FCC's job is to assess indecency complaints based on the content of the offending broadcast, not by a scorecard of how many people might be offended.

A key reason for more media consumers not complaining about offensive content, however, is that they don't know where and how to impact the system. The FCC has now made it simpler for citizens to file content complaints. Unlike in the past, when complaints had to be in writing and provide transcripts and/or audio-video evidence of the material, the FCC now allows for online submission at www.fcc.gov.

Complainants simply go to the Enforcement Bureau section of the menu and access Form 475B through the "Broadcast Complaints" link. The form asks for information about the time, date, and channel of the broadcast in question, and allows space for comments and descriptions. Transcripts and audio-video evidence are not required, although the FCC is happy to receive such evidence. If the citizen does not have the audio-video material, the FCC now expects the broadcaster to provide it as part of the review process. The process is very simple now, so even the most mindless couch potato can file his protest with the FCC.

It is time for those audience members who represent the community standard to step forward and make their voices heard. Otherwise, the Hollywood "standard" is left unchallenged.

# CHAPTER FOUR

✌

# This Is Not News

It has been said that news is the conversation of democracy. If that is true, our democracy could be headed for trouble. That is because much of what passes for news in the broadcast journalism industry just doesn't qualify as news and is not worthy of conversation beyond the most superficial context.

The news media establish the agenda for what topics the public will consider to be important and thus worthy of our society's collective attention. This flow of information is essential as the citizens in a democracy engage each other and their elected officials to manage the nation's business. For those many citizens who rely most heavily on television news for determining the nation's agenda, they know more about celebrity scandals, bizarre crimes, and cute animals than they know about their kids' schools, the management of their tax dollars, the economic conditions of their community, and so forth. This sort of warped agenda does a disservice to the citizenry and demonstrates a shirking of broadcast journalism's constitutionally created duty to serve as information gathering surrogates for the public.

In spite of some audience erosion caused by the Internet and general loss of interest, news consumers still rely on television news as the prime agenda setter of the nation. A recent Harris Interactive poll showed that 77 percent of the population regularly watch local television news broadcasts, and 71 percent tune in to the network news, well ahead of newspapers, radio, and the Internet. Other studies by the Pew Research Center and the Radio-Television News Directors Foundation (RTNDF) confirm that local television is, indeed, the major source of news for consumers. But while the people are still watching, their collective judgment is that their broadcast news professionals are not serving them effectively. Eighty percent of RTNDF survey respondents are critical of local television news for its undue profit motives and desire to report a story first. Six in ten viewers believe TV stations avoid stories that are too complex, and 77 percent believe broadcast journalists chase sensational, easily promoted stories even when the news value of such stories is minimal.

During a speech in the early 1990s, former Federal Communications Commission chairman Alfred Sikes chastised television newscasters for being preoccupied with their own celebrity status and focusing too much on the notion that "good pictures equal good journalism." He warned that "the norms and habits of TV news now threaten to undermine our collective ability to respond as a nation to the most serious problems we face." He pointed out the heavy responsibility of broadcast news, and scolded broadcasters by saying, "Our primary news source leaves our democracy disabled." Now, a decade and a half later, with even more media emphasis on the visual and the bizarre, Sikes must really wonder if our nation can respond to complex issues such as drug abuse, moral decay, educational underperformance, immigration, and so on. Challenging issues can't be confronted when the dialogue begins with local television setting an agenda filled with irrelevance, simplicity, and emotion.

A report issued in 2000 by the Shorenstein Center on the Press, Politics and Public Policy at Harvard University warned that changes in the news coverage landscape could be "weakening the foundation of democracy by diminishing the public's information about public affairs and its interest in politics." The study found that soft news, defined as being focused on the sensational, personality-centered or entertainment news, had increased from less than 35 percent to about 50 percent in less than twenty years. Professor Thomas Patterson, the author of the study, warned that the softening of the news by editors and producers trying to maintain audiences might actually be having the opposite effect: "Over the long run, soft news is shrinking the number of viewers and readers, especially because those who prefer hard news are much heavier consumers of news." The study asserted that interest in public affairs and political news was declining because of the focus on soft news and the overall negative tone of what political news was disseminated. This audience drift can hardly be good for a nation that relies on informed citizens to elect its leaders and guide policy with its societal sentiment.

Other studies have confirmed that the focus in journalism has shifted over the last two decades from an emphasis on policy, politics, ideas, and analysis to the current agenda of scandal; personality; human interest; entertainment; and spot-news cop-shop stories of crime, wrecks, and fires. In most local television news markets, stories about crime outnumber stories about government and policy by a more than three-to-one margin. Of course, certain crime incidents are newsworthy, but the imbalance suggests to the audience that crime news is twice as important as public policy news. In reality, most crime stories have little broad impact and affect only those people immediately involved and those in the vicinity. It is little wonder that people who are heavy viewers of local television news are more likely to overestimate the amount of actual crime in their communities, the so-called mean world syndrome expressed by communication researcher George Gerbner.

The saddest aspect of the misguided news agenda being set by "professional" news decision makers is the warped perception of reality that is relayed to the public. Legendary broadcaster Walter Cronkite once said it was the news industry's job to hold up a mirror, so the public could see what is really happening. When the public looks into this broadcast news mirror today, it does not see the issues that affect them and relate to their daily lives and priorities. Instead, it too often sees the latest update on Britney Spears's kids, or minutes' worth of live coverage from a fire or crime scene with no broad application to the viewers. The godfather of the broadcast news industry, Edward R. Murrow, once told fellow broadcasters, "To be credible, we must be truthful." That line applies not only to the accuracy of each individual story, but to the importance of the stories selected to be put on the community's news agenda. Citizens now deciding to not watch television news, in all likelihood, are leaving the audience because they simply don't see the news lineup as a truthful representation of the world they live in.

None of this is to say that all news must be serious and deal with policy complexities all of the time. Indeed, there is a role in news storytelling to profile interesting people or show lighthearted slices of life. Audiences love what newscasters call "kickers," those light features that end a newscast. The world's events are not all gloom and doom or heavy policy matters, so telling about life's happier moments or human interest stories is certainly part of holding up the mirror to society. This is a matter of balance—providing news that fairly represents the newsworthy in our society, both good and bad. That balance is too often out of whack, as indicated by studies that show almost 30 percent of local television news time is devoted to crime news and only 2 percent devoted to stories about education. Think about the disservice this lack of education reporting does to our community, given the importance of education for every family, every employer, and every taxpayer in the community, not to mention that the effectiveness of education today affects the crime statistics of tomorrow.

Veteran broadcast correspondent Brian Wilson of Fox News Channel believes the news agenda should be broken into thirds—one-third of news devoted to things the media must tell (breaking news, gas prices going up, etc.), one-third of the news devoted to things the media should show (school board policies, local economy, etc.), and the remaining third being things the media want to tell (features, fun stories about pop culture). This breakdown seems workable if applied by sensible producers who understand the events of the day and the makeup of their audience. The formula, however, doesn't work when the balance of the "want to tell" invades the "must tell," or when the "must tell" is determined to be a Michael Jackson update or a grandstanding politician making outlandish statements. Even the best-intentioned formulas rely on the application of sensible news judgment.

## Traditional Criteria for News

The criteria for determining news have been outlined consistently over the years in journalism textbooks. They are as follows:

- High impact—Events or developments that affect a large number of people, whether they want to be affected or not. Things like increasing utility costs, inflation, and severe weather are all high-impact events because they affect the lives of virtually everyone in the audience. News stories about the latest twist on *Survivor* or the latest celebrity scandal are not high impact.
- Conflict—Opposing forces that shape events have the element of conflict. Conflict creates change, and a changing landscape is newsworthy. Legislative debates, elections, courtroom trials, and social debates like abortion and immigration rights all represent newsworthy conflict. Not all conflict is necessarily bad. The civil rights movement saw much debate and conflict, but much good was eventually accomplished. News stories about petty, partisan political bickering are not necessarily news, even if the remarks are inflammatory and divisive.
- Timeliness—Events that are "new" are newsworthy, as common sense would indicate, but everything that just happened is not necessarily newsworthy. Television operations too often overemphasize "live," "late breaking," and "this just in" for developments that just aren't relevant or important.
- Proximity—Events that are geographically close to your viewing area are newsworthy, of course. It makes you wonder why local television stations are prone to show car chases, wildfires, and building implosions from thousands of miles away.
- Prominence—People who are well known make news. That is because prominent people like government officials or corporate leaders make decisions that affect our lives. Other prominent people, like professional athletes or entertainers, are of interest to us because we enjoy their performances. This news category, however, is inflated in the eyes of many news producers who think audiences care more about these individuals than is warranted. Is every pronouncement or appearance by Tom Cruise or Paris Hilton newsworthy?
- Human interest—The human experience can often be understood or appreciated by the stories of common people doing uncommon things. Acts of heroism or altruism might affect very few people, but they can serve to help inspire us or give insight to our

fellow humans. There is, indeed, a place for human interest reporting, but not at the expense of the "must tell." In addition, effective human interest reporting does not include reporting about
the bizarre and freaky. It is not important for us to see X-rays of a
guy's skull with a nail in it or the five-legged calf romping in the
barnyard.

Separately and collectively, these criteria make sense when applied by
news producers focused on their audiences and not their budgets or outside pressures. Events that might qualify as news should be measured
against these criteria. The most newsworthy events would be those
matters that have a legitimate degree of several of the criteria, but any
more than that only seems to matter in the theoretical world of the academic textbook. Too often, now, the news gets defined by out-of-
touch news producers based on a false sense of timeliness, contrived
conflict, exaggerated prominence, and even falsely asserted impact.

## Reasons behind the Warped TV News Agenda

None of this is to suggest that producing a sensible news agenda is easy.
It isn't. News directors and producers at local television stations, not to
mention network newsrooms, have countless inputs to their decision-
making process from public relations firms, government offices, police
scanners, and so forth. Deciding under deadline pressure what is important enough to make the limited time of a newscast is not easy. That's
not to say it can't be accomplished effectively. Regarding basketball of-
ficiating, legendary basketball coach Norm Stewart of the University of
Missouri once acknowledged that being a basketball referee was difficult, "but it shouldn't be impossible, either." And so it is with making
news judgments. It is a difficult job, but it shouldn't be impossible. It
does take insight, expertise, an understanding of the audience, and an
appreciation for the societal obligation that goes with the job.

One must ask why it is that news producers around the country can
lose their collective compasses and veer off into making decisions to air
news of little consequence or impact, playing it safe by following false
industry standards. One reason is surely the pressure that comes with

having to cover and update news in today's twenty-four-hour news cycle. The constant need to get new stories on the air and to do so quickly in the heedless attempt to beat competitors to the air leaves little time for reflection, research, and preparation. (By the way, hurrying to get stories on the air first is a largely wasted effort since the average viewer wouldn't even know which station got to the air first with any particular story . . . or care.) The television industry mantra that there is a news deadline every minute exaggerates this pressure and no doubt leads to going on the air without adequate background or with stories that simply aren't that relevant and deserving of the title "breaking news." Think of how often you see a television station go live with a late-breaking story to the scene of a crime or traffic accident, only to have the reporter announce that he or she doesn't have important details about the situation the station couldn't wait to announce. Also, notice how often broadcasters break into programming with "news alerts" on matters that just aren't essential for us to know immediately. Cable network news is most susceptible to this constant deadline pressure, but so too are broadcast networks and even local stations, which feel false competitive pressure and are looking for ways to fill as much time as possible when such "opportunities" present themselves.

Another reason for the warped agenda we too often see is that television is generally considered a medium of emotion, and it does poorly trying to relay information. Thus, producers cave in to this tendency of television, looking too often for what makes "good television," relying on visual images that help us emote rather than inform us. In a day's news cycle, video of emotion can always be found at the crime scene or the philanthropic event. Information, however, is frequently found in budget reports, government documents, statistics, court records, academic research, or test scores. That information takes time to ferret out, to analyze, to understand, and to present intelligently. Further, information-based stories seldom have ready-made video and certainly not emotional video to carry a story. Thus, because emotional video is easier to come by and packaging information into interesting video is so challenging, it is no wonder we see more stories that represent the producers' vision of "good television" over stories that might represent good journalism.

Finally, resource limitations of personnel and the limitations of the technological resources play into making the television news agenda what it is. Local television news operations have relatively few reporters compared to the local newspaper. Further, television reporters are expected to produce one or more news packages per day, and seldom are given time to research stories or do long-form reporting. The occasional exception is for multipart reports designed for sweeps ratings periods. Filling the news lineup is very much a day-to-day mentality, with the focus on "spot news," stories that come up and can be covered on the day of broadcast, with little continuity provided in future days' broadcasts. The technological resources, while great from an engineering standpoint, ultimately limit and warp the coverage of news on routine days. Jet copters and live satellite reporting trucks are great for covering floods, hurricanes, and stories that demand the immediate coverage and perspectives that they can produce. On days when such stories aren't in the mix, however, the urge to use live equipment and airborne visuals overcomes sensible news judgment. News executives feel compelled to use the fancy technology frequently because the equipment is paid for and must be justified to higher management. There is also the false notion that audiences are impressed somehow with "live via satellite" (they aren't) or aerial views of scenes that could be shown just as well from ground level. Check out any week's worth of local newscasts to see how often stories are done live or from the air with no apparent time or content rationales.

## This Is Not News!

Because of the reasons outlined above, the consuming public ends up with an agenda of items that just are not newsy by any sensible standard. The weaknesses in the television news industry combine to operationalize for us an agenda that too often focuses on easy-to-find, disjointed, hit-and-run, irrelevant side shows and not enough on news of substance, impact, and necessity. Consider the amount of television news time devoted to the kinds of topics described below, and then assess how important the information was for you to know and whether your life would have been adversely affected by not knowing it.

## Shrill Voices

Whether from the Left or from the Right, speakers who want to be in the news spotlight well know that their chances to get on television and make "news" go up when they make strident comments. Despite all of the reasoned and well-articulated potential news sources in the public arena, it is the shrill among us who can most effectively garner airtime. Former entertainer Harry Belafonte is by now a footnote to the entertainment industry, but he maintains a profile in the news media through his extreme remarks. In recent years, Belafonte has called President Bush "the greatest terrorist in the world," compared the Homeland Security Department to the Nazi Gestapo, and characterized then secretary of state Colin Powell as a "house slave," among other wild expressions. Way too often, the broadcast news media legitimize and give a podium to such polarizing rhetoric by broadcasting the remarks and then following up with analysis and even interviews. CNN blessed the Gestapo remark by granting Belafonte a prime-time interview to rant further. NBC's *Meet the Press* raised Belafonte's incendiary remarks in a discussion with Illinois senator Barack Obama, as though there weren't enough other important issues to discuss with a sitting senator.

Oliver Stone is an accomplished filmmaker. What he thinks about filmmaking and the film industry is worth noting. His opinions on American foreign policy, however, are likely no more insightful than those held by the next guy at the bar. Still, when Stone blasted President Bush while speaking at a film festival, the Associated Press gave national distribution to the remarks. Stone said Bush's policies had set America back ten years. He said he was "ashamed" for his country. Had Stone merely been discussing film or had his comments been more moderate in tone, nobody, including the Associated Press, would have cared to disseminate them.

Conservative broadcaster and former presidential candidate Pat Robertson was given ample broadcast coverage of his strange proclamation about assassinating Venezuela's president Hugo Chavez. Minister and activist Jerry Falwell generated news when he suggested the terrorist incidents of 9/11 were related somehow to the nation's moral decline.

Entertainers often feel compelled to speak out on political issues, even though their expertise and background have nothing to do with the issues about which they speak. Should anybody care or have their opinions influenced by what Barbra Streisand, Rob Reiner, Natalie Maines, or any other singer or actor thinks about any matter other than music or movies? Of course not, but that doesn't stop broadcast news interviewers from giving credence to these self-indulged and uninformed voices, just as though average citizens should take note.

The electronic media eagerly broadcast every promotional outburst of shock jock Howard Stern. Sure, his radio fans like him, but most everybody else is not interested and doesn't need to know about Stern's business dealings, moral reflections, or ideas about the First Amendment. Still, Stern's rants about the Federal Communications Commission and his move to Sirius satellite radio were widely covered by television, including lengthy feature interviews on cable news programs and even on the venerable CBS newsmagazine 60 Minutes.

When it comes to legislative news, moderates and compromisers are left out of the sound bite wars, but the polarizing voices on both sides of the aisle always get plenty of time. The outspoken politicians are the ones who most likely jump in front of microphones, but that is no reason for broadcasters to give them airtime. Instead of letting Democrats like Chuck Schumer, Dick Durbin, and Nancy Pelosi throw bricks, how about getting a more reasoned dialogue from Joe Lieberman? Instead of hearing partisan Republican rhetoric from J. D. Hayworth and Newt Gingrich, let Richard Lugar explain things.

This concern is not about censoring the voices of the shrill; this is about journalistic judgment and making decisions about how best to inform the public about the political issues of the day. The voices of the shrill can still shriek, but without the amplification of the broadcast world.

## Bizarre Events Involving Attractive Young Women

This will come as a shock to all local and network television news producers around the country, but the sad stories of Natalee Holloway, Laci Peterson, Jessica Lynch, runaway bride Jennifer Wilbanks, and any other weird event involving attractive young women should not count as "news," even if the audience does have a sick curiosity about the circumstances surrounding these women. Although the events surrounding these women could all make for powerful mystery novels, there is no broader significance to their stories for anybody not immediately associated personally with these individuals. Think of how much news time has been devoted to topics such as these in recent years.

Sure enough, audiences will watch the breathless updates on these real-life dramas and that's how news producers justify their continued oppressive and intrusive coverage. The ratings of Greta Van Susteren's Fox News Channel program *On the Record* surged to the top of cable news in summer 2005 once Greta started going wall-to-wall with Natalee updates. But giving the audience what it wants and creating a sensible news agenda of substance are two different things. Audiences will gawk at personal tragedy because news producers tell them these events are important. The sad circumstances of individuals, however, should not give license to media producers and their gawking audiences to trample the personal dignity of victims for ratings and vicarious drama.

The media frenzy surrounding the false confession of weirdo John Mark Karr to the murder ten years earlier of little JonBenét Ramsey is yet more evidence of a news industry driven to deliver emotion over substance. Broadcast producers bombarded viewers with extended updates about Karr and ran segment after segment rehashing the murder of JonBenét, of course accompanied by video and photos of the cute little girl. News teams analyzed and overanalyzed the inflight menu of Karr as he traveled to the United States from Thailand, and showed jet copter video of the jail exit that Karr *might* come out of when it was time to move him to Colorado. Never mind that forensic experts were roundly dismissing Karr's fake claims almost from the minute he "confessed."

These kinds of stories have no "high impact," and further blur the lines between news and entertainment. The television news industry, however, trumpets coverage of such events with slick graphics, promotional announcements, and thematic music. They splash the coverage of these women with smiling photos of the women in happier times. One must question whether these stories would be so appealing to the news producers if the women involved weren't so photogenic. Likely not. The emotional sadness these stories deliver to the audience is not sufficient justification to keep promoting them. The murder of Laci Peterson and her unborn child was a horrible event, but as law enforcers well know, the prime suspect in any pregnant woman's death is the father of the unborn child. Police will also note, sadly, that this circumstance is not that un-usual. The disappearance of Natalee Holloway makes every parent fear-ful for the loss of their child, but police blotters around the country have cases of missing children. Jennifer Wilbanks is not the first woman to get cold feet about an approaching wedding, even if her method of calling off the ceremony was bizarre. Jessica Lynch is to be saluted for the sacrifice she made for her country, but she was one of thousands who have made similar or greater sacrifices during the Iraq war.

Physical appearance is clearly a factor in deciding to provide jour-nalistic coverage of these unusual stories involving young women. Take the case of young, blonde middle-school teacher, Debra LaFave, who entered the national spotlight in 2004 when she got arrested for hav-ing sex with a fourteen-year-old student. The deluge of coverage at that time was excessive and unnecessary, given the lack of wide impact on anybody beyond the devastated families. Then, unwilling to let the matter drift away, NBC's Matt Lauer took the sensational story to a ridiculous level in September 2006 with his "exclusive" interview with LaFave. Never mind that the teacher was arrested in 2004 and sen-tenced to house arrest in 2005, Lauer and NBC shamelessly extended LaFave's media limelight with an interview that was highlighted on the *Today Show* and during prime time. LaFave wasn't the first and hasn't been the last schoolteacher to have sex with a student, but her physi-cal appearance clearly makes her more newsworthy to prospective in-terviewers like Lauer. Lauer even asked LaFave if she thought her case was receiving so much attention because she was pretty! Of course, that's exactly why Lauer was there. The interview provided no broader application to any news angle and will be remembered largely for LaFave's statement, "He wanted it. And yeah, I gave it to him."

Beyond the unnecessary intrusion into the private circumstances of these individuals, the overdone media coverage of such cases always seems to spin off weird sideshows that also hit the spotlight. Scott Pe-terson's grandstanding attorney Mark Geragos became a household name for his courthouse theatrics. Pornographer Larry Flynt first en-tered the media limelight after the Jessica Lynch rescue by claiming he had topless photos of Jessica from a predeployment party, and then a few days later as he patted himself on the back for deciding not to pub-lish the photos over concern for Jessica's image.

Personal tragedy should not qualify as news without a broader application to the public interest, which should be clearly explained. It is that simple.

## Celebrities in Trouble

Nothing revs the television news motor more than a celebrity with legal trouble. Although these stories have little overall effect on anybody and thus provide limited value as news, the coverage of celebs going through the legal system is splashed all over cable and local newscasts, and even highly profiled in the early evening network news agendas. The coverage is characterized by breathless live updates from the courthouse, aerial helicopter video of celebrity motorcades, endless analysis and legal speculation from "experts," and excited commentary from fans at rope lines. Sadly, this kind of coverage creates the apparent merger of traditional and tabloid news. Audiences are told by mainstream newscasters that this kind of coverage, formerly the stuff of tabloid newspapers or television, is essential for them to know. It isn't.

Sure, prominence is indeed a factor in determining what is news, but prominence alone is an insufficient factor when the stories have no importance beyond the curiosity angle created. Look at the coverage in recent years of Michael Jackson, Martha Stewart, Kobe Bryant, Rush Limbaugh, and Robert Blake, and see if any substantive elements can be found. Beyond the freak show nature of these cases, little news can be presented that really informs an audience or goes beyond mere titillation. Did the audience really learn anything about the national problem of child molestation by simply following the Jackson case? Did the nation learn anything about corporate business shenanigans and their effect on our economy by following television coverage of Martha Stewart? Was anything learned about prescription medicine dependency by the media coverage of Limbaugh? What opportunity there might be for giving these stories a broader significance and application is generally lost in covering the peripheral details of the situations— what Martha was wearing in the courtroom and how her hair was done, how many minutes it took for Jackson to get from his home to the courtroom, the effect of Kobe's problems on his next shoe endorsement, and so forth.

News producers will say that the audience really wants to know about the goings-on of these celebrities. Is that because these celebrities have so many fans? Or because those fans really care about these celebs beyond their entertainment value? Or is it because the media have convinced our culture that celebrity news is so important because the media have chosen to show it to us?

## Lottery and Gambling Stories

If the jackpot gets bigger than usual in any state's lottery, it's a sure thing that local television news outlets will not only let you know about it, but also lead the cheering. In this sense, television reporters leave their roles as disseminators of information and instead lead the story with emotional and exciting proclamations.

When the multistate Powerball lottery reached near-record levels in the winter of 2006, newscasters in one Indiana market went into overdrive, not only to report on the lottery, but to promote its excitement. One station opened its reporting with the male anchor exclaiming, "The city is getting pumped up about the Powerball," followed by the female anchor saying, "It's huge!" The on-screen graphic read "Powerball rally" as the anchor went on to say, "Hoosiers have extra luck on their side. There have been thirty-three major jackpot winners in Indiana—the most of any state." Of course, there is no legitimacy at all to the "extra luck" claim, given the randomness of lottery numbers. Another station led its coverage with the anchor declaring there was a "Powerball frenzy" and showing on-air a handful of lottery tickets he said had been purchased by the staffers in the newsroom. The narration added, "The big bucks are luring even nongamblers into playing." That newscast ended with the station's "Picture of the Day," a video segment of a lotto machine printing off tickets for that night's drawing. Yet another anchor led the lottery coverage by blaring, "There is a lot of excitement in the air" in front of a graphic that said, "Huge Jackpot." The anchor then tossed the story to a reporter live on the scene of a convenience store, where the field reporter got live comments from grinning lottery players about what they would do with the winnings.

Free lottery commercials, of course, continue when the winners are actually announced at highly orchestrated state-sponsored press conferences that are made for television. The formulaic coverage then includes live reports from the scene with beaming winners talking about what they'll do with the money and proud lottery officials talking about the fun of seeing the winners and how much lottery revenues help the state.

Lottery news, of course, is not really news by any sensible standard. The people who play are playing voluntarily and monitor the jackpot sizes without the promotion of the news organizations. As a percentage of the viewing audience, the number of people playing the lottery in any given week, even with big jackpots, is relatively low, so high impact is not a factor. But whatever minimal value could be justified by news producers to cover the lottery as important news, there can be no justification for using a news show to do shameless hype for the lottery, a gambling activity that can easily be questioned on moral grounds.

## Routine Crimes, Fires, and Traffic Wrecks

Most news coming out of the cop shop has little or no impact on anybody other than the people immediately involved. Most house fires, domestic disturbances, car wrecks, and even shootings and localized crimes have little application or long-term significance to the average audience member. That's not to say that these events aren't important to the unfortunate people who suffer from them, just that these examples of human suffering should not qualify as news for everybody else to absorb. Television news operations, however, can't resist the urge to cover these events, frequently with live reports from the scene. That's because there is a steady supply of such stories in most markets and they are easy to cover. In addition, there is usually "good video" of the flames, firefighters in action, banged up cars, grieving family members, perpetrators being paraded by the police, emotional eyewitnesses who get to be on television, and so forth. In fact, the accessibility of video and the opportunity to go live are factors in whether these events sometimes get covered in the first place. The house fire or shooting aftermath not captured by video might well not even get a mention in the news.

In so-called news that borders on the ridiculous, local stations often show car chases or warehouse fires from areas of the country far removed from their own viewers. Cable news channels will also show these chases or other sensational video even though virtually nobody in a national news audience is affected by the incident.

Of course, the problems associated with fire safety, neighborhood crime, traffic hazards, and so forth do affect large numbers of people. The isolated, episodic manner of covering these matters, however, does not help the audience at large understand the problems except by inference and causes media victimization of the people who have already suffered from being unwillingly put into these circumstances. The audience learns little about the causes, effects, and ramifications of domestic violence by a spot-news treatment of one family's troubles. The audience learns little about crime patterns or causes by spot coverage of the two-bit holdup of the convenience store, whether the culprits are apprehended or not. Presenting coverage of a dozen traffic wrecks in isolation fails to help audiences understand the nature and implications of these mishaps, if there even is any. Broad context is needed to have these stories be of any relevance to the audience at large. Absent that context and insight, these stories frequently are told from the standpoint of audiences gathering to collectively gawk at somebody else's misfortune, under the guidance of lead gawkers in the television news world.

### "News" about Prime-Time Network Entertainment Shows, Movies, Concerts, and Book Releases

Many people enjoy watching prime-time television programs like *Survivor*, *Lost*, *American Idol*, and so forth. What happens on these shows, however, is not news. That doesn't stop television news from taking up valuable news time with updates on the shows, interviews with the performers, and chats with fans. Surely, the channels and magazines devoted to pushing popular culture can be found by those dedicated fans who crave this information. The message news broadcasters send by lowering the standards of news programs to air such fare is that these prime-time shows should be important to the daily lives of average viewers. Such content in news broadcasts is solely a crass attempt to promote other programs on that channel in front of other audiences.

The pop culture as news initiative doesn't end with prime-time television shows, but extends to movie openings, concerts, and book releases. Live reports are aired from outside movie theaters any time a promising new movie release arrives in town, along with canned prerelease interview material with movie stars on their promotional junket.

It is always "news" when the local concert venue announces its upcoming concert schedule and then again on the day that any midlevel singer or guitar player shows up in town. Again, the opportunity for live reporting is irresistible to news producers who interview fans waiting in line for tickets or to enter the concert arena. Each new Harry Potter book is "reported" live from bookstores, with video of kids dressed up like characters and bookstore managers talking about the excitement of the release.

## Anything Else with Odd Pictures to Fill the Time between Commercials

If there is a police car chase anywhere in the country, odds are it will be shown (perhaps even as it happens!) in each television market in the nation. If there is a building implosion anywhere in the country, it will also be shown with a news anchor lead-in saying, "Look at this!" If there is a tornado, or a flood, or large hail, or a snowstorm anywhere from coast to coast, you will see it on your local television newscast. If an animal does something unusual or is found somewhere it is not normally found, chances are you will see it in your newscast, as though it had anything to do with your life.

In this era when satellite distribution of video is easily accomplished amongst various news services, weird video shot by professional or even amateur videographers anywhere in the country can make it to your channel in minutes. Of course, there is no relevance for viewers in Ohio to be seeing a tornado on the Kansas prairie. The lives of Californians are not affected by a police car chase in Florida. And pretty much nobody needs to see the water-skiing squirrel or the capture of the traffic-stopping beaver in Baltimore . . . unless you like watching *Animal Planet*. Surely, there is no real harm in wasting airtime showing the occasional severe weather outbreak from another region or the out-of-place furry animal, but the frequency of such "news" reports does raise the question about whether this stuff is really so important and if there really is nothing else of substance to report. Tornados are a common sight on the plains each spring, and each newscast a half continent away doesn't need to show them. There are car chases every day somewhere in the country, but apparently they only count as news if a television jet copter is around at the time. Without the video, a police chase in Poughkeepsie is suddenly not newsworthy. News consultants instruct producers to find at least one animal story for each newscast. Thus, producers each day scan the video services looking for the bear in the tree, the moose in the neighborhood, or the dog that has ducklings following it.

## The Need for Better News

Clearly, the television news hole on any given day is filled with the kinds of wasted coverage described above. Our ability to fulfill our civic duties and perform in a democracy is not enhanced by a barrage of celebrity news and news of the bizarre, irrelevant, and offbeat. Although it is, indeed, difficult to provide in-depth and insightful news coverage at all times, too often the news is filled with the marginal because it is easy to get. No enterprise or deep investigation is needed to wait near the police scanner for the next fire, traffic wreck, or two-bit holdup. Celebrity trial coverage is generally delivered on a platter to reporters by publicists and attention-hungry lawyers. In short, it is convenient and easy to get stories from the wells that never run dry and require little heavy lifting. Every day provides video of severe weather somewhere in the country, or a police chase, or a new animal at some zoo. That's why our news is so formulaic, routine, and, at times, irrelevant to the lives of viewers. If the readily available, easy stories were eliminated, think of how brief the average local or even cable newscast would be.

In a speech to the Radio-Television News Directors Association in 2004, award-winning reporter Ted Koppel told about the times earlier in the history of television news when news departments weren't expected to be profit centers. He said at that time "editorial decisions really were made on the basis of what the news managers perceived to be the most important events of our time." The pressure now, of course, both at the network and local levels, is for news operations to turn a profit. Sadly, that motivation appears to have altered the gumption of the broadcast journalism industry and pandered to perceived audience whims. The profit motivation, however, need not be a cause for deterioration of standards. The viewing public might well be willing to watch serious, relevant news that doesn't focus too often on the sensational and peripheral. The dumbing down of the news might well be a cause of audience drift; as Koppel has speculated, "When we began taking our journalism more lightly, people began taking us less seriously."

Television news producers and their consultants will blame the audience for the news agenda, saying they are only giving the audience what it wants. To blame the audience, however, ignores the basic fact that it is the news producers who have responsibility for what goes into the newscast and that viewers seldom know what stories are in the lineup at the time they tune in. Viewers mainly choose to watch "the news"—however it is defined that day by the producers. Most sensible viewers will watch news of substance and relevance, if the industry has enough respect for viewers' intelligence to give them the chance.

None of this discussion is designed to overgeneralize and suggest that broadcast news doesn't often have shining moments. Much good work is done by many hardworking professionals. That good work, however, is too often overshadowed by the poor judgments and concessions to "entertaining" news. Our communities, indeed our democracy, demand that the excellent work be more common than the pedestrian.

# CHAPTER FIVE

$\mathcal{S}$

# Television News or MTV?

Legendary television journalist Daniel Schorr worked many years at CBS and was a key figure in the development of CNN as a legitimate television news operation. He has been a participant in much of the history of television news. But he doesn't like the manner in which television news now operates. In remarks to a professional media organization, Schorr accused the television news world of blurring the line between fantasy and reality: "It is a world where a journalist, forced to use the tools and techniques of entertainment, finds reality under constant threat in the ceaseless effort for something more dramatic, more confrontational and more violent than what happens in real life."

Indeed, "the tools and techniques of entertainment" have infiltrated the television news process, further confusing an audience that has a relatively low awareness of the workings of television. One must question whether the media help or hinder our collective ability to learn what is really happening in the world, and whether television news is trying to dazzle us or inform us. When a news reporter narrates a story "live" from the scene of an event that took place hours ago, do we see the techniques of entertainment being used over the need to portray reality? Are flashy on-screen graphics and dramatic music used to enhance our understanding of the news or to just show off production gymnastics? No doubt, the audience expects a degree of "viewability" in the newscasts they watch, and using up-to-date technology and production capabilities can make sense in providing information to an audience. The techniques of entertainment, too often it seems, have steamrolled sensible journalistic judgment to the point where the production of news looks more like the production of a music video, leaving audiences trying to differentiate between fantasy and reality. Too often in television news, packaging trumps journalism.

While news directors complain of budget constraints and lack of news staff, television executives spend gleefully on jet copters, newsroom sets, graphics packages, production music, tower cams, and newfangled weather radar systems that are indistinguishable from the old ones. Some news operations now have invested in mobile news vehicles that can transmit live pictures to the air while on the move. Now somebody must figure out which stories need to be covered with a live camera in a car that is careening down a street. To date, such mobile car cameras seem to be only suited for driving around and transmitting live pictures of snowy roads, as though a stationary shot or a taped version of snowy roads wouldn't suffice. Jet copters are more likely used as flying promotional vehicles for their respective stations than for any sensible journalistic purpose. A jet copter might well be useful in a journalistic sense on a handful of occasions per year, but the copter is used on a near daily basis to justify the investment to ownership. Thus, we see aerial video of scenes that could be just as easily shown from the ground.

Media theorist Marshall McLuhan coined the now famous phrase "The medium is the message," suggesting that the communication medium in use itself delivers an effect beyond whatever content is transmitted. In a sense, the television news world, too, is developing a notion that it is the technology of the news that creates an effect, with the actual content of the broadcast being secondary. Thus, the television news world, with its emphasis on the staging, production, and technology of news, has shifted focus and meaning away from the ideas and issues that news should be disseminating.

Television news executives apparently believe that news viewers can be generated and the competition can be topped by dazzling audiences with slickly produced newscasts with a heavy focus on high tech. Of course, it is unlikely that consumers wanting real news are impressed by news glitz over substance, but that's the way the game is played in today's television news world. Audience members need a better understanding of how the processes of news production impact the content of their "news" programs, thus becoming better positioned to determine whether they are actually being informed by the news or just impressed by the production ambiance.

## "Live" for the Sake of "Live"

Certainly, the ability of television news reporters to go "live" with news that is really breaking is a tremendous asset for the medium. News consumers need and want the latest developments on a story. Just as certainly, however, average news consumers can tell the difference between stories that really merit a live report and those for which the *live* label is merely concocted. A false sense of urgency, a false sense of importance, and a false sense that a story has new developments are created when news producers have reporters go live on location just for the sake of being live. News consultants tell their media clients that live news sends the audience a signal that the television station is on top of things and gathering new details right up to the moment of broadcast. But seriously folks, as Bob Hope would say, how many viewers really think that news is actually breaking each day right at 6 and 11? Further, how many viewers really think news done on the fly is as accurate and carefully presented when done live? Additionally, this false sense of live urgency falls into the ridiculous when, after a "live" introduction, the video presentation shows footage that was clearly shot and edited long before the "late-breaking" setup. The news formula in use today, however, demands that field reporters be live on location, whether or not the circumstances dictate. That's why we see reporters standing roadside when reporting on traffic matters, or reporters standing outside during a snowstorm while telling people not to go outside.

A good deal of academic research sheds light on the misguided phenomenon that is live television news reporting. Researchers C. A. Tuggle of the University of North Carolina and Suzanne Huffman of Texas Christian University coordinated a study in which they viewed countless newscasts from eight television markets of varying sizes. In content analysis, the researchers determined that there were more live than taped reports, and that there was no identifiable journalistic reason for live reporting in nearly 90 percent of all such reports. Further, the research revealed that most live reports were done from what are called "black holes," locations where the reporter is announcing live, but the event or news associated with that location is long finished. Such black-hole reporting is frequently done in front of vacated city halls, where a city council meeting was held earlier in the evening and everybody has since gone home. Other black-hole reports are aired from street corners where accidents or crimes occurred earlier, but where no follow-up action continues. Even more ridiculous are the occasional live field reports where correspondents are literally standing outside the television station itself, just to create the appearance of being on location. The study also found that most "live" reports are actually just "donuts," in professional terminology, where the reporter does a live introduction, but simply to introduce a videotaped package that was clearly produced earlier. Perhaps the most sobering result of the study, however, was that the most common subjects for live reporting were entertainment, sports, and human interest stories—hardly the kinds of stories that deserve the emphasis and sense of importance that live coverage suggests.

A study by Rut Rey of Iowa State University looked at audience reactions to reports coming out of the invasion of Iraq in 2003. Rey compared audience information processing of live reports from Iraq versus packaged reports. No differences in content understanding were found between the group of viewers who saw live reports and the group that saw packaged reports, thus calling into question the sometimes cited rationale that live reporting somehow enhances audience reception.

In a national survey of television reporters and news directors, Tuggle and Huffman found that television news professionals do, indeed, acknowledge that going live for the sake of live reporting was a frequent and often unnecessary practice. A wide majority of respondents agreed that live reporting does exaggerate the news value of a story beyond what it deserves from a journalistic standpoint, but that pressure from management and outside news consultants keeps the practice in place nonetheless.

None of this discussion is designed to suggest that live reporting should not happen or that the appropriate use of the latest technology isn't valuable for viewing audiences. It does appear, however, that the overuse and misleading use of live reporting when it is not warranted is an intellectually dishonest practice being employed by the television news industry. When such practices are used more for promotion or glitz, the audience is misled and underserved, and the lines of entertainment/fantasy and reality are further blurred. Award-winning television journalist Ted Koppel of *Nightline* fame expressed a key perspective on live reporting during a speech in 2004 to the Radio-Television News Directors Association convention: "We delude ourselves into believing that by simply focusing a live camera on an event, and dropping in the occasional ad lib, we are committing journalism. We're not."

Even in the coverage of legitimate stories that really are breaking, going live doesn't necessarily serve the audience, the people involved in the news event, or the emergency personnel at a breaking-news scene. Viewers of live coverage in Los Angeles several years ago witnessed a distraught man set his truck on fire on a roadway and then commit suicide for an audience of thousands. A spokesman for the offending station explained that the station had no way of knowing that the man would take his own life on camera. Well, duh. But that's why going live in such emergency situations, when there is no opportunity for editing, is an unwise journalistic decision. Emergency personnel in such situations as threatened suicides, hostage situations, and police chases view live media coverage as a complicating factor in bringing the events to a safe conclusion. And beyond generating sensationalism, no purpose is served by media intrusion into the personal turmoil of these matters.

## Man on the Street

A standard convention of television news, fueled in large part by the consultants who travel the country giving high-priced advice, is to get input on virtually every story from the common people. These interview snippets are called MOS, or man on the street, by the television news professionals. Sadly, of course, most stories don't lend themselves to MOS comments, but that doesn't stop the practice. The formula pushed by consultants and management dictates the use of MOS comments, so in they go.

The function of a newscast, it would seem, is to provide audiences the information they need to know to conduct themselves as citizens of their community. Taking up valuable newscast time to get passing observations from the average Joes or Josephines of the town hardly enlightens anybody. Further, MOS comments are hardly representative of what the average person is thinking anyway. Input is gathered only from those people who happen to be handy and are willing to spout off in front of a television camera, hardly the cross-section of society that might make this exercise valid.

A viewer who wants to know what the commoners think on any particular issue should be able to gather such opinion from discussing that issue with friends, family members, or coworkers. There is little need to tune in the news to have this public discussion function served.

Perhaps the worst aspect of MOS, however, is that the average citizens are frequently asked to provide perspectives on matters for which they are not well backgrounded. How many average people are in a suitable position to provide commentary on legislative matters, legal matters, or economic matters? While it is true that everyone is entitled to his or her opinion, all opinions are not created equal and all are not equally worthy of broadcast airtime. Thus, as average people take up broadcast time with off-the-wall reflections, the comments and insights from informed analysts and experts are diminished or missing altogether. Audiences are not served effectively by this practice, despite the assertion from broadcasters that grassroots input informs the audience. To get a sense of how enlightening it is to be getting news insight from MOS, check out Jay Leno as he does his *Tonight Show* segment called "Jaywalking," and see whether you want your news analysis from the common man. Frankly, a prime reason for television reporters to use MOS is that gathering it is easy, and it fills a lot of air time with minimal research or verification.

## Video News Releases

Video news releases (VNRs) are packaged public relations reports that look and feel like real television news stories. They are prepared and distributed to television news outlets by public relations firms or corporations on behalf of clients, with the specific intent of getting into broadcast news programs. Government agencies have even engaged in this practice. The packages can be aired as provided or can be adapted for voiceover narration by local television announcers using scripts that are supplied. Thousands of such reports are prepared each year and made available to television stations via satellite, digital transmission, or videotape distribution. Many stations refuse to use such offerings because of the obvious ethical implications that these "reports" are not independent journalistic offerings and are instead sales or public relations pitches disguised as news.

While it's difficult to know how widespread the use of VNRs really is, a report by the Center for Media and Democracy (CMD) provides evidence that the practice of television news operations using VNRs is maybe not as isolated as professional broadcast journalists have asserted in recent years. The CMD tracked just thirty-six such VNRs over a period of ten months and found that these reports ended up on a total of seventy-seven television stations around the country, in both large and small markets. Clients getting exposure in these "news reports" included such corporations as General Motors, Pfizer, and Capital One. The CMD reports that in each case where a VNR was used, the offending television station failed to disclose the source of the material, a clear violation of Federal Communications Commission (FCC) rules.

FCC commissioner Jonathan Adelstein reacted to the CMD report by blasting the television news industry for "a betrayal of the public trust and the law." He pointed out the obvious ethical issue involved, saying, "The problem with the many video news releases . . . is that they lead viewers to believe they are watching a real news report when instead they are getting a subtle dose of corporate propaganda."

The CMD report prompted an FCC investigation into the use of VNRs. In August 2006, the FCC sent letters of inquiry to seventy-seven broadcast licensees asking them to explain whether they had properly disclosed the sources of VNRs aired on their stations. Again, Commissioner Adelstein took the lead on the issue, stating at the time of the investigation announcement, "The public has a legal right to know who seeks to persuade them so they can make up their own minds about the credibility of the information presented."

Television stations use VNRs because they are readily available and they fill airtime cheaply. Some might even be on topics of interest to the audience. None of this, however, excuses broadcasters from the responsibility to clearly inform the audience of the source of the story topic, its information, and the canned video. Most stations would rather not provide these on-air disclosures, simple as this might be, because of the shame that comes with admitting the station is being manipulated for PR (public relations) purposes and hasn't done its own independent reporting. The broadcasters would rather continue blurring the line between fantasy and reality. In so doing, news executives are comfortable letting the audience slumber in its ignorance, hoping nobody finds out otherwise.

Literate viewers should be on the lookout for "news" reports that deal with new medicines, electronics, the automotive world, or any new and trendy product. They should consider if they are watching a report independently produced by a local journalist or if they might be seeing a PR package parading as news. Even if they see a local reporter introducing and narrating the report, the piece might still have VNR elements if corporate logos are prominently displayed, exterior locations are not from the station's geographic area, or the expert interviewees are not identified by a local professional affiliation. Refer to your local phone book to see if the medical doctors, scientists, or engineers shown on-screen are even from your area. If they aren't, odds are that material was provided from outside your television station's area through a VNR.

## Walking and Talking and Using Props

Television news consultants constantly tell on-air reporters to get involved in their reports by moving around, pointing to things, holding objects, and so forth. This advice has little to do with journalistic reporting but a lot to do with imposing production values of television into the news. No doubt, news through the medium of television has to be provided in a manner that is viewable and visually interesting . . . and that's not easy. As Fox News Channel anchor Brit Hume once said, "The problem with television is so much of what we do every day is the translation of news into television form." But making television news viewable from a production standpoint must still keep the presentation of information foremost and shouldn't stoop, as is often seen, to gimmickry and off-the-wall displays of reporter activity. News directors bemoan the decline of the news audience, but maybe the audience is just departing because the content of news programs bears so little resemblance to real news.

Exhibit A for displaying the utter foolishness of staging TV correspondent involvement in their stories came in October 2005. NBC reporter Michelle Kosinski was reporting on the flooding in New Jersey during a live segment of the *Today Show*. Kosinski was shown paddling a canoe in a flooded area. "It's really tough to control a canoe or a boat when you're out in it," she told the audience. About that time, however, two men walked into the camera shot in front of Kosinski, the water barely above their ankles as they walked through the scene. To be sure, the area had been hit hard by flooding, but just as surely, the production of this report was designed more to show Kosinski supposedly battling the elements than it was to give an accurate sense of the event.

Reporters frequently are seen "walking and talking," as the producers call it, doing their narration while walking down a sidewalk or across a snowy lawn. They are encouraged by producers and consultants to be active; thus we see reporters handling gas hoses while reporting on gas prices, reporters stooping to pick up debris after a windstorm, or reporters holding snow shovels when reporting about snowy weather. A reporter once signed off a report about a heat wave by jumping into a pool. Another report about hot weather had the reporter sitting poolside with her legs paddling the water.

While good reporting might on occasion need to demonstrate a process or show objects, most stories don't really need the correspondent to create silly action or to bring props from the theater stage. Viewers should scrutinize correspondent movement and props to determine which are needed for understanding the story and which amount to stagecraft that blurs reality.

## Parasocial Interaction and Happy Talk

The news is presented to us by human beings, and we want to be informed by people we view as personable and professional. For many news viewers, their impression of the newscaster is the determining factor in which channel's newscast they choose to watch. Many audience members are not well suited to judge the writing skill or journalistic judgment of news organizations, but they can easily decide which people they want to watch deliver the news. The most-watched newscasters develop with audience members a sort of "through the screen" relationship that is labeled by some researchers as "parasocial interaction." Parasocial interaction is a sense of connection or friendship with favorite media personalities believed by audience members to be likable and similar to themselves. That's why television stations work so hard to promote their news personalities both on and off the air.

But while it makes sense for news organizations to push the personalities of their newscasters as a way to attract viewers, many news managers have the false sense that this parasocial relationship can be artificially created and manufactured with clever newscaster banter, strained laughter, and wardrobe manipulation. Newscaster relations with viewers, however, are based on audience perceptions that the announcer is genuine, credible, and sincere—all factors that can't easily be faked. Further, viewers most likely to develop parasocial interaction with newscasters are motivated to do so initially by a genuine interest in the news itself and by a sense that the news presentation was realistic.

Sadly, news managers try to concoct positive newscaster-viewer relations with a strategy that has nothing to do with news content or authenticity. First, producers force happy talk amongst the on-set announcers, making lighthearted conversation about all kinds of disconnected matters on the way to introducing a field reporter, the weathercaster, or just going to a commercial. Put a stopwatch on the amount of time devoted in any newscast to anchors wishing each other well, endlessly thanking the field correspondents for their fine work, introducing the weathercaster, and thanking viewers for watching. This banter frequently features forced chuckling and laughing, sometimes just moments after telling about murder and mayhem.

A current strategy to make on-air news personnel seem conversational and active is to have the anchor engage the field correspondent with a follow-up question. These questions, as most anybody can tell, are designed in advance and are simply scripted interrogations. The ruse was given away on air by a Midwestern television station recently when the anchor was trying to ask his question of the field reporter and got his tongue tangled up, finally just blurting, "Do you know what I am trying to ask?" The reporter smiled on camera and said, "Of course, because I wrote the question for you." This advanced planning makes sense on one hand because it relieves the anchor of having to think up sensible questions on the fly and avoids the possible awkward situation of the anchor asking a correspondent a question for which the reporter doesn't know the answer. But why the fake scenario? What is lost if the reporter just includes the follow-up information in the original report and the anchor goes from there to the next topic?

Another recent staging strategy at many local stations is to have anchors or reporters teasing upcoming reports with live updates from the newsroom. In these orchestrations, the anchor is shown at his newsroom desk with the backdrop of the working newsroom. The anchor will sometimes engage other reporters about what they are working on for the next half hour. Male anchors in these setups don't wear their suit coats and like to have their shirt sleeves rolled up in order to create the impression that they are hard at work in the trenches. While doing solid journalism can be hard work, it's not like these guys are swinging sledgehammers in the newsroom. Such staging is unconvincing and unnecessary. No viewers really think that the desk work of a news anchors is so physical or messy that the anchor's sleeves must be rolled up.

Faked or forced personality doesn't work, can be detected by the audience, and ultimately diminishes credibility because blurring reality with the personalities in the news impacts the reality of the content of the news. How often did we see contrived conversation and forced laughter from Walter Cronkite or Ted Koppel?

## On-Screen Crawls

One need not be a psychologist to know that even alert people can only grasp so much information at any one time. Then take average audience members, many of whom are doing other things while trying to watch the news, and try to figure what television news organizations are trying to accomplish by running on-screen crawls. This practice has more to do with pushing an image of hip modernism than with informing audiences. In particular, the crawls are designed to appeal to younger news audiences and get them interested in the news, the assumption being that young adults raised in an era of computers and multitasking can process the on-screen video and the wordy crawls at the same time.

Much academic research has focused on the limited capacity of audience members to receive multiple inputs while processing mediated messages. Basically, if you are paying attention to the newscaster, you are missing the crawl's information, and the other way around. Trying to go back and forth between the messages, which are not synchronized in any way, likely leads the viewer to misunderstand key elements of both stories. While news managers insist that viewers like the crawls and that the motivation is simply to provide more information, research indicates that the practice is not helpful from the standpoint of informing an audience and its only possible benefit is image promotion. Researchers Lori Bergen and Tom Grimes of Kansas State University, along with Deborah Potter of the NewsLab, conducted experiments that concluded that viewers cannot effectively process parallel messages at the same time and likely lose some meaning from the message they focus on because of the distraction caused by a competing input. Further, in spite of the common wisdom about younger viewers being able to handle multiple messages, the research showed the young viewers to be no more efficient in processing information than the general population.

Thus, crawls might produce a trumped-up sense of ongoing urgency, but their utility is generally nil, particularly when the crawled headlines are filled with fluff and routine news items.

## The Atmosphere of Excitement

From bold on-air pronouncements to bouncy music to quick video edits, newscasts have surely taken on the feel of entertainment programs. No wonder cerebral viewers who want to see real news are tuning away. What they see looks less and less like an information program. News anchors barrage viewers with screeching proclamations like "Look at this!" "Exclusive!" "A story you will see only here!" "Team coverage!" and "You won't believe this next story!" Graphics blare, "News Alert" and "Breaking News" for routine stories or old stories with a minor new detail surfacing. Every second of airtime spent teasing upcoming stories is less time for news content. Every production effort spent with razzle-dazzle is less newsroom focus on issues.

The pacing of news presentation has picked up with interview sound bites shrinking in duration. Even for political election stories, sound bites of presidential candidates on network newscasts are just over seven seconds, hardly enough for a comment, let alone an explanation or a complete thought on an issue.

News videography is making quicker edits and using more creative camera perspectives in an effort to increase emotional arousal of viewers and, in particular, attract younger viewers. A team of researchers led by Annie Lang of Indiana University, however, found that standard, slower news video production practices that match audio and video, use silence on occasion, and use chronological narrative style increase information recall by viewers without losing viewer attention or emotional arousal. Another research team, led by Maria Elizabeth Grabe of Indiana University, compared viewer responses to the more flamboyant production practices associated with tabloid news (music, slow motion, flash frames for transitions, etc.) to standard news packaging. This study indicated that the tabloid production practices did, to some extent, increase the emotional arousal of viewers. The tabloid practices, however, did not help viewers in retrieving information from the reports, which should be the primary factor of a news package. Further, viewers rated news packages prepared according to a standard news style to be more informative and credible. The overall thrust here is, frankly, that viewers have a limited capacity to absorb information at any one time, and throwing too much excitement, dazzling edits, and quick-paced material at them in too short a time accomplishes nothing but confusion. Fast pacing and clever video techniques might work fine for Hollywood effect and music videos, but the supposed goal of a newscast to provide relevant information is not served by such practices.

Surely, the packaging and presentation of news can't be stodgy and boring, but overreaching to create fake excitement and unnecessary music video–style pacing and visuals comes off as insincere. It also makes for an atmosphere more focused on entertainment than information. This likely turns off the true news viewers without enticing anybody not already interested in real news.

## It's Time to Reinvent Television News

The focus on responsible journalism is too often overwhelmed by the values of the entertainment world, slick marketing practices, and an obsession with using technology. Noted television correspondent Christiane Amanpour of CNN has condemned the content of television news as "demeaning, irrelevant, super-hyped sensationalism." She told a conference of professional broadcasters, "No matter what the hocus-pocus focus groups tell you, time has proven that all the gimmicks and all the cheap journalism can only carry us so far."

The general manager of WDRB-TV in Louisville, Bill Lamb, criticized the television news industry in an on-air commentary in 2006. He specifically blasted the gimmickry of labeling too many stories as "breaking news." He blamed the trend on news consultants and the temptation of competing stations to copy each other. He compared the practice to crying wolf and said, "Lying to viewers is no way to get them to watch." He said such gimmicks threaten the credibility of all broadcast news stations. He has instructed his newsroom to only use the breaking-news setup when a story really is big and really is happening at that moment. Surely, television news needs more leaders like Bill Lamb.

For television news to meet its potential, the producers in charge must change the standard practices and conventional wisdoms currently in place. This will take guts, no doubt, because newly designed newscasts won't look like the stereotypical ones of today that have become virtual parodies. The new practices must focus on unblurring the lines between fantasy and reality. Most important, a redesigned approach to television news must show a respect for the special duty journalists have in informing the citizens of a democracy.

# CHAPTER SIX

ॐ

# Packaged Politics

The mass media play a complex and controversial role in the nation's political conversation. Journalists and broadcasters help determine the key "issues" on which a campaign will be decided. Candidates rely heavily on the skill of media consultants who can create advertising messages that sell the candidate to the voters. Politicians play to the media lights to spin messages, promote causes, and bash opponents. Talk radio and political television pundits exaggerate sensitive issues into controversies in order to generate ratings. It doesn't take much to ignite a political firestorm in a media world that is in constant overdrive. The heightened pace of political discussion in the 24/7 news cycle leaves little time for reflection and reasoning. Competitive journalists and power-hungry politicians all want to use the media to their advantage, exploiting the emotional nature of mediated messages to confuse, scare, shock, and sometimes mislead audiences who don't work hard enough to sort through the smoke.

It's not the actual television, radio, newspaper, or Internet media that confound the political process, of course, but rather the manner in which the prominent players have chosen to use those media in framing the national dialogue. The superficiality of much political discussion, the emotionally charged political advertisements, and the frequent hostility exhibited in the political realm take advantage of the characteristics of the media, particularly the electronic media. The media, of course, only process the messages put into the pipelines by the image disseminators. It is clear, however, that all political strategy and political news coverage is designed by the key players with an eye to how their messages will be affected by the media conduits transporting those messages.

## "News" Coverage of Political Campaigns Leaves Voters Poorly Informed

News coverage of political campaigns has been criticized in recent years as superficial and too focused on the "horse-race" aspects of the campaigns. A study of the local news coverage of the 2004 campaign demonstrates that these criticisms are well founded. Most Americans rely on local television newscasts as their primary sources of information. When it comes to political information, these Americans are sadly uninformed.

Researchers at the Lear Center at the University of Southern California, along with researchers at the University of Wisconsin, analyzed the evening newscasts in eleven representative markets around the country for the twenty-nine-day period leading up to the 2004 general election. They reviewed the content of all news broadcasts aired between 5:00 p.m. and 11:30 p.m.

What the researchers discovered is disturbing, to say the least. Less than two-thirds of all half-hour newscasts contained even one election-related story. If it weren't for the presidential race, that figure would have been lower. In 2002, less than half of all newscasts had at least one political-election story. The presidential campaign of 2004 increased the amount of political coverage, but took the air out of coverage related to any state or local races. Sixty-one percent of all political stories focused on the presidential election. While the presidential election is, indeed, important, local viewers can access information on that process through network broadcast or cable outlets, whereas local broadcast news stations could provide local political news that wouldn't be featured elsewhere in the television world. Only 8 percent of all newscasts had a story about a truly local race, defined as U.S. House, state legislature, or regional offices.

The study found that a typical half-hour local newscast in the month before the 2004 election contained only three minutes and eleven seconds of campaign coverage, less than the time devoted to crime and accidents. An average campaign story was eighty-six seconds in length, but a sound bite from a candidate was featured in only 28 percent of the stories. Compounding the lack of candidate sound bites is the fact that these sound bites averaged only twelve seconds in length.

Of the campaign stories to hit the air, only 32 percent dealt with issues. Forty-four percent of all campaign stories covered horse-race issues like polls, campaign strategies, and candidate travel schedules. Most of the remaining political stories covered the voting process and voting locations. Research by Professor William Benoit at the University of Missouri focused on network and national newspaper coverage of the Democratic primary race of 2004. His study found that 66 percent of that coverage focused on horse-race content and only 12 percent on candidate policy positions.

Only 1 percent of all news stories in the Lear Center study analyzed campaign ads of candidates. Thus, viewers in the markets studied would see more time devoted to candidate commercials in any given evening of viewing than they would news coverage of the candidates.

More disappointing results emerged from research of the 2006 election season. Researchers at the University of Wisconsin's NewsLab analyzed early and late evening local newscasts from five Midwestern states over a one-month period beginning after Labor Day, the time when campaigns enter full swing. They found that the average 30-minute local newscast during this one-month period contained only 36 seconds of election coverage. Only 56 percent of the newscasts studied had even one election story. And predictably, election horse race and strategy stories outnumbered coverage of issues by almost a three to one margin.

The overall lack of coverage in the days leading up to an important election is disturbing. The weak focus of that coverage is also disappointing. It can be easily inferred from these results that news directors simply don't think their audiences are interested in or will watch news about politics. The audience might well deserve part of the blame, but the viewers aren't leading the decisions about what stories get covered in a news broadcast. The challenge for these news directors, if they can be coaxed into serving their duty as audience surrogates serving the information needs of the citizenry, is to make political coverage more interesting and relevant. Horse-race stories, of course, are easier to get and produce than issue-based stories, but likely don't interest viewers who aren't political junkies. Doing the journalistic research to differentiate candidates on key issues will be more time-consuming and difficult than taking candidate PR (public relations) releases or listing candidate travel schedules. Making the issues concrete enough to make them real for average citizens is also challenging, but necessary.

Audience members might tell station focus groups that they are more interested in coverage of traffic accidents than election stories, and grade school kids say they'd rather eat candy than vegetables. Responsible school dieticians still feed the kids broccoli. Television news directors need to give the audience what is needed, not what is necessarily more convenient or even what the audience says it wants. A study commissioned by the National Association of Broadcasters (NAB) in October 2004 found that 42 percent of viewers thought local broadcasters were spending *too much time* covering local elections. Given how little time was actually being devoted to election news, according to the Lear Center research, this NAB finding might really be judging the approach to election news, not the actual amount of coverage.

Political coverage in newspapers is widely considered more thorough and issue based, but in an era when less than 15 percent of media consumers rely on newspapers as their primary source of news, this still leaves many voters unprepared to cast intelligent votes. It is up to television, particularly local television, to contribute more effectively to the election information process. Some politicians, like Arizona senator John McCain, responded to the Lear Center study by criticizing broadcasters for their lack of local political coverage, even threatening legislation to hold the broadcasters more accountable for public service obligations. Such legislation seems to run contrary to having independent media voices, but broadcasters would be smart to recognize that the concern for effective political news coverage is real.

## Mediated Political Debates and Their Limited Utility

Theoretically, putting political candidates on the same stage to debate the issues before a broadcast audience is a great idea. Sadly, however, as exemplified by televised presidential debates over the years, these events are generally of little consequence. Of course, in a really tight campaign, a great performance by one candidate *could* provide the essential edge to win over enough undecided or wavering voters to win the election. More often, it seems, these debates see very little actual debating and instead a lot of posturing, spinning, and playing to the television cameras. Candidates and their PR handlers see to it that genuine debate and exchange does not happen. That would be far too risky compared to "staying on message" by simply repeating segments of stump speeches, boilerplate partisan remarks, or cute one-liners. A candidate's priority is simply to avoid the major gaffe, not to make rational, debating points. For these reasons, the electorate is poorly served by the debate structures and strategies currently in place.

Television is the major reason for these generally ineffective debates. Television is a medium of emotion and provides information inefficiently. Thus, style is more important than substance in televised debates, a fact campaign handlers well know and exploit. The obvious contrasts of John Kennedy's appearance and gestures to Richard Nixon's are legendary. Viewers of the 1992 debates probably recalled little of the argumentation, but much was made of the first President Bush looking repeatedly at his watch while Bill Clinton performed for the cameras. In 2000, audiences could hear Al Gore sighing every time George W. Bush spoke. Viewers might not follow complicated political issues, but they can easily decide whose mannerisms and personalities they prefer.

Sure, some past presidential debates have impacted the campaign results, but effective debating had little to do with it. Jimmy Carter said he wouldn't have won the 1976 election had it not been for the debates. That might be true, but surely Gerald Ford's blunder in which he declared there is "no Soviet domination of Eastern Europe" had more to do with the election outcome than Carter's debate technique. The tables were turned on Carter in 1980 when a polished and performing Ronald Reagan frequently repeated his one-liner to Carter, "There you go again." Misstatements or consultant-designed one-liners should not be turning presidential elections.

The 2004 presidential debates between George W. Bush and John Kerry were predictable and unimpressive, partly because both are poor public speakers but mostly because they came off as canned and overly scripted. Virtually every Kerry response included a phrase like "I have a better plan" or "My plan is better." He pointed out at every opportunity that Bush "chose the wrong way" or had made a "colossal error of judgment." Bush, for his predictable part, kept saying, "Stay on the offense" and "We'll continue to do so." Of course, it's hard for a candidate to really put together a developed case when he is limited to two-minute responses to questions and ninety-second responses to questions directed at the opponent. But that's the format preferred by the sound-bite world of television producers, not to mention the candidates themselves, who can avoid really explaining things while dancing around for two minutes at a time.

Presidential debates have lost their viewing appeal for voters over the years. The Reagan-Carter debate in 1980 had over 80 million viewers. Presidential debates in election years 1984, 1988, and 1992 averaged over 60 million viewers. Presidential debates in 1996 and 2000 averaged barely 40 million viewers per event. The three 2004 debates between Bush and Kerry averaged about 53 million viewers, boosted by an estimated audience for the first debate of 62 million. This modest viewership increase in 2004 over the previous twenty years was likely because this was the first presidential election after the 9/11 attacks and subsequent war on terror. Of note are the poor viewer numbers for the second (46 million) and third (51 million) debates.

It might be just as well that many voters don't bother to watch the presidential debates. A good television debater would not necessarily make a good president. There is little transferability from grandstanding in a television debate to managing a cabinet, being commander in chief of the military, and doing hard bargaining with congressional leaders.

These events are not really debates in the traditional sense, by the way. A true debate would feature the candidates arguing their different views on a particular proposition that would provide equal challenge for both. These made-for-television events are really just, in a sense, dueling press conferences with the topics and questions being guided by journalists/panelists. Those journalists should be asking questions more in the style of a debate proposition and not target questions specifically to one candidate or the other.

Journalists aren't used to asking such balanced questions, so we end up with press conference–type questions. In the first 2004 debate, questioner Jim Lehrer of PBS asked Kerry, "Do you believe you could do a better job than President Bush in preventing another 9/11-type terrorist attack on the United States?" Besides the fact that this is a yes-no question that gives no direction for elaboration, how is Kerry supposed to respond to this type of query? Lehrer later asked Kerry, "What colossal misjudgments, in your opinion, has President Bush made in these areas?" Such a question surely plays into Kerry's hands, setting him up to launch into a boilerplate campaign rant. Bush also received imbalanced questions, for example, "Are there also underlying character issues that you believe are serious enough to deny Senator Kerry the job as commander in chief of the United States?" Debate questions should be focused on issues and worded such that each respondent is equally challenged.

Voters who want to be informed about what happens in televised political debates would be better served by reading a published transcript the day after the event. Whether they watch the debate on television or read a transcript, voters should focus on candidates' comments that distinguish them clearly from their opponents. Ignore the majority of the material on which the candidates agree. They all love their country, want a good economy, are tough on terror, and like apple pie. See if the candidates have concrete plans or supporting material to back up their campaign slogans. Further, see if the candidates can directly answer a direct question from a panelist. Candidates frequently ignore specific questions and just fall back on prepared statements, regardless of what is asked of them. Look to see if the candidate can generate any spontaneous thought. Look for genuine sincerity to go with the concocted emotions and slick talk planned in the practice sessions with consultants.

Finally, voters should ignore the postdebate punditry, which focuses almost entirely on who "won" and who "lost" the debate. A debate winner is not necessarily the best candidate. The best debater might not share your values or priorities. Evaluate the candidates' performance on your own and cast your vote accordingly, regardless of what media experts say about the debate's outcome.

## Political Ads Are Annoying, but Play a Key Role

Everybody likes to say that they hate political campaign commercials, but the utility of such commercials indicates those commercials are here to stay. Campaign advertising allows candidates to reach a broad range of the electorate and get messages to prospective voters who wouldn't ever know about a candidate from in-person contact or even news coverage. Advertising allows candidates to initially define and explain themselves, to later criticize or challenge opponents, and then, if needed, to defend against the attacks of the opponent. Advertising is used not only to generate awareness and win undecided voters, but also to shore up current supporters and mobilize them sufficiently to get them to the polls.

Of course, candidates and their strategists know that television advertising is the key to getting their messages out. No matter how much print or billboard advertising a candidate does or how many pins or bumper stickers the individual hands out, a candidate will not be viewed as a legitimate political force unless she or he is seen in television commercials. Television is the medium that distinguishes a candidate as a legitimate contender. Television ads send a strong rhetorical signal to the electorate and opponents that a candidate is worthy of consideration and has the financial punch to contend. Further, no medium can reach as many and as varied an audience as television.

Critics of television advertising in the political world say that such ads don't really change anybody's voting preference and that voters really don't learn anything from slick, thirty-second commercials. While it is true that most voters will not be influenced by the commercial packaging of politicians, it only takes the swing of a few voters to change the outcome of close elections. It is these susceptible voters who campaign commercials seek to influence. Research evidence suggests that it is the least politically aware voters who are most likely moved by impressive campaign commercials. The votes of these generally unaware voters count just as fully as the voters who follow politics closely, and no politician is going to turn down the opportunity to reach even the politically disinterested. That's why many campaigns put on a late TV advertising blitz in the final hours of a campaign. These less-engaged citizens have to be reached on their terms. That means running the campaign commercials during prime-time entertainment programs or whatever programs are being watched by the unaware voters.

The negative tone of much political advertising is not appreciated by many viewers and analysts, but that doesn't stop candidates from running negative ads. That's because negative ads often work. Negative ads allow a candidate to rhetorically define and label his opponent and get out information on that opponent that otherwise might never surface. Negative ads demonstrate that a candidate is aggressive and willing to engage the political battle. Negative ads help to solidify a candidate's most ardent supporters. The active followers of a candidate would lose heart if they felt their preferred candidate didn't have the courage to take on the opposition rhetorically.

A common assumption is that negative political advertising turns off voters and makes them less likely to vote and otherwise participate in the political process. Analysis of the relevant research by Professor William Benoit of the University of Missouri indicates, however, that negative advertising doesn't ultimately diminish turnout. He suggests that while some voters might well become disenchanted with the negativity and opt out, other voters watching negative ads become agitated enough to roust themselves to go vote. From the standpoint of an individual politician, of course, it's all about winning the election. If one candidate can capitalize on a rough-and-tumble, negative campaign and turn off that portion of the electorate least likely to support him, then attack advertising is a practical strategy, even if the smell of incivility permeates the election season.

Finally, a major downside to political advertising, particularly on television, is its enormous cost. The potential contamination of the electoral process by forcing candidates to grovel for money is a concern, as is the notion that the winning candidate is likely the one who spends the most. The preoccupation of candidates with campaign fund-raising and the general expense of media campaigns in this era has led to the many efforts by interest groups and Congress to limit campaign spending and set strict rules for donors. These limits are difficult to implement while at the same time keeping First Amendment free expression rights intact. Citizens donating money and candidates spending it on advertising are free expression gestures generally protected by the First Amendment.

## Bloggers Impact the Political Process

They certainly aren't mainstream by any means, but political bloggers on the Internet have begun to make an impact on the political landscape. Bloggers are the new voices of the grassroots public, trying to play their role in the national dialogue. Access to traditional media outlets is generally limited to the politically and/or financially privileged, but now anybody with a laptop can get his musings, reflections, and rants into the Internet blogosphere. Bloggers serve a key First Amendment function in creating an electronic town hall. They play a role in helping to establish a national agenda, telling the big shots in the political and media world what is on the public's mind. This can only be healthy for democracy.

A key function of bloggers is that they watch the mainstream media like hawks and hold the mainstreamers accountable for their mistakes. In the 2004 election year, the discredited story about supposed National Guard memos and President Bush was barely off the air before bloggers at the Right-leaning freerepublic.com website posted challenges to the story's accuracy. Bloggers also pointed out inaccuracies in the CBS story about a secret plan to reinstate the draft. The Left-leaning talkingpointsmemo.com blog jumped on Fox News Channel (FNC) during the campaign for posting inaccurate quotes on the FNC website attributed to Democratic presidential candidate John Kerry. In 2006, bloggers caught Reuters news agency using doctored photos of bombing damage caused by Israeli air attacks on Hezbollah targets in Beirut. Earlier, while the mainstream media looked away, blogger anger helped push Trent Lott to resign his Senate leadership position after Lott made awkward comments at a birthday party for Strom Thurmond.

Postelection research by the Pew Research Center after 2004 showed that 11 percent of the nation's voters read political blogs during the election season. The more popular political blogs were receiving up to 8 million visitors per month during the height of the 2004 campaign. This figure will likely be higher in future election cycles as citizens become more active on the Internet and bloggers become more visible.

It's not uncommon now for political bloggers to be interviewed on talk radio or cable news shows. Political parties now cater to the blogging world and have given some of them credentials to cover party conventions and other party activities. Advisers inside the 2004 presidential campaigns acknowledged that they monitored blogs to see which issues were getting traction and to assess the political analysis going on.

The mainstream press generally doesn't like these political bloggers. Interestingly, however, many regular media outlets now have their own reporters doing blogs. But the renegade bloggers are a threat to the regular press, removing the monopoly on immediate and mass-produced political analysis and commentary. Editors and producers at the mainstream media have bashed bloggers because there is no system of checks and balances on what goes into the blogosphere. Mainly, it seems the traditional press just doesn't like "outsiders" playing a role in determining the nation's news agenda.

The traditional press points out that most bloggers don't have specific training in journalism, as if the First Amendment requires any such thing to post analysis and opinions. Some bloggers, however, have a great deal of formal education, surpassing most journalists in this regard. Josh Marshall at talkingpointsmemo.com has a doctorate in history. Glenn Reynolds of instapundit.com is a law professor. Blogger Duncan Black is a former economics professor. Markos Moulitsas of dailykos.com has a law degree. While not all bloggers have such backgrounds, the blogging world is not just made up of random goofballs. Besides, how much journalistic training does one need to have a legitimate opinion and the right to post it?

It is true that blog readers should scrutinize blog content carefully and not buy into everything posted without putting things in context and doing some credibility checking. Many blogs are highly partisan. Citizens who read blogs should have other things on their political reading menu, including the more traditional broadcast and print media sources. Blog readers should be sure to separate the facts from the opinions on the websites. Very little blog material consists of actual research or original reporting, although some sites will link to original data or research. Readers must also keep in mind that some opinions are more worthy of consideration than others. In the blog world, all opinions are surely not equal in value, and the incivility expressed in some blogs is a concern. Blogs with uncivil rhetoric and personal attacks have the least to offer in terms of reasonable dialogue.

Bloggers have been granted legitimacy as real journalists deserving free press protections through recent government decisions. The Federal Election Commission (FEC) decided in spring 2006 that bloggers will receive the same media exemption to criticize or promote politicians as do newspapers and will not be subject to restrictions imposed by campaign finance laws. The FEC decided to leave as unregulated all Internet political activity except for paid political ads, which will still come under campaign spending laws. Thus, bloggers can link from their sites to the campaign messages of favored politicians or forward a campaign's press materials to readers. A California appeals court has also sided with bloggers in defining them as journalists under the state's shield law. That law protects journalists from being forced to reveal the sources of their information. No doubt there will be many future decisions as to whether bloggers are to be defined as journalists with free press rights, but the early indications are promising for the blogging world.

## The Media World Spotlights Uncivil Political Discussion

While lack of civility has often characterized the political process throughout history, the overwhelming media world of today seems to intensify and enlarge the uncivil tone of politics in the current generation. The result is increasing polarization and, for many citizens, disengagement. The information and rational analysis citizens need to make decisions on important issues is upstaged in the media by grandstanding politicians and political operatives calling names, pointing fingers, and throwing rhetorical brickbats. Journalists and talk show hosts pander to the harshest of voices, leaving the voices of sanity, compromise, and civility on the sidelines.

From Vice President Dick Cheney telling a senator to "f*** himself" to former vice president Al Gore shouting at the top of his voice that

President George W. Bush "betrayed" the country, there are numerous examples of political leaders setting poor examples of how civil political discourse should be conducted. The media not only jump to report and rereport the most strident of politicians' remarks, but also add to the harsh atmosphere with outbursts of their own making. Talk radio hosts from the Left and Right fuel audiences with their disgust for people who have different political views. Cable television talk shows too often have hosts and guests interrupting each other and shouting accusations at each other. Instead of slotting a moderate analyst to make sense of controversial issues, cable news segments frequently feature sharp-tongued, highly partisan Democratic and Republican strategists for the obvious goal of creating a divisive confrontation. Levelheaded discussion is not likely when the media schedule talk show guests they know will launch rhetorical grenades. NBC got just what it wanted when Air America radio host Al Franken came on the *Today* show and opined that White House staffers Karl Rove and Lewis Libby should be "executed."

In the smack-down world of political media, it's no wonder politicians and pundits alike feel compelled to answer harsh challenges with more harsh challenges. Senator Hillary Clinton couldn't resist taking a shot at conservative author Ann Coulter when Coulter's book included criticism of the politics of some women who had lost husbands in the 9/11 attacks. Clinton called Coulter "vicious" and "mean-spirited." In turn, Coulter responded, "I think if she's worried about people being mean to women she should have a talk with her husband," and then went on to name one of Bill Clinton's accusers.

The immigration debate sparked by the media in 2006 featured more name-calling and accusations than it did analysis or problem solving. Radical spokesmen from both sides of the issue were rounded up and herded onto the national television stage to label border security proponents as racists and xenophobes and open-border proponents as anarchists and bleeding hearts. Coverage of the issue focused on the emotional images of the mass demonstrations and whether Republicans or Democrats could capitalize on the issue for the midterm elections. Surely, immigration reform is an emotional and divisive issue, but the focus on the more flammable aspects of the matter surely diminished the opportunity of the more rational politicians to promote compromise and effective solutions through legislation.

The harsh voices come from both the Left and the Right. Liberals Franken, political strategist James Carville, radio commentator Randi Rhodes, and others combat conservatives Coulter, talk show host Michael Savage, and radio commentator G. Gordon Liddy, lining up followers who surely become less likely to consider alternative views. The personalities and rhetoric of these pundits at times overshadow the arguments, even relevant ones, they wish to make. The emotional clout of the broadcast media elevates the status of these shrill voices. The producers and programmers who allocate airtime for these voices legitimize their scorched-earth rhetorical style. In such a climate, can any minds be changed? Or do minds just become irretrievably closed? The health of America's political process hinges on the answers to those questions.

A generation ago, ethicist Karl Wallace of the University of Illinois promoted rhetorical guidelines for political discussion. These guidelines emphasized a focus on relevant issues, avoidance of distortion, removal of emotionally loaded language, and concern for public versus private gain. America's media consumers should use these guidelines to measure what they see and hear from so many of the visible pundits that crowd our political talk programs. When side issues get heavy traction and get discussed with excitable and charged proclamations, it is likely private gain is being sought at the expense of public good. In these many cases, civic-minded media consumers should look elsewhere for their political insights.

In his inaugural address in 1961, President John Kennedy spoke of the challenge of easing international tensions, saying, "Let us begin anew, remembering on both sides that civility is not a sign of weakness." Those politicians, pundits, and media producers who delight in explosive, divisive, tough-guy rhetoric should ponder Kennedy's words.

## The Government's Attempt to Regulate the Media's Role in Campaigns

Since the earliest days of broadcasting, the government has seen fit to involve itself in how the electronic media affect political campaigns. The Communications Act of 1934 contained two key federal political broadcasting laws that still apply today. Section 312 requires all broadcast stations to provide reasonable access to federal political candidates to get their messages out. Federal candidates are those running for the U.S. House and Senate, vice president, and president. This access is generally through advertising but can include public affairs broadcasts, debates, and other programs. Section 315 of the act requires broadcasters to provide "equal opportunity" in the use of broadcast airwaves by political candidates for any office, federal, state, or local. Of course, the First Amendment prevents any such access or leveling-the-playing-field sorts of laws from being applied to newspapers or other print media. Newspaper publishers could, at their discretion, not provide any access to their pages for candidates, or could provide free space to promote candidates they support.

Broadcasters, however, in that they operate on publicly owned airwaves, are subject to federal oversight. The government justifies such regulation of political broadcasting based largely on the "impact rationale"—the notion that broadcast radio and television messages have the power to potentially alter elections and that all candidates must be treated fairly in terms of access to broadcast airwaves.

Section 315 is sometimes referred to as the Equal Time Rule, but that designation is actually misleading. The law requires broadcasters to provide *equal opportunity*. Thus, if one candidate for office has more funds and can buy more political commercials on a particular station, that station is only obligated to provide the opponent the opportunity to buy that amount of time. The advertising time provided to candidates for the same office must be comparable in terms of potential audience size. For example, a broadcaster can't play favorites by selling a preferred candidate advertising time on top-rated programs and sending the opponent's commercials to poorly rated, overnight shows. Broadcasters are also required to sell this political advertising time to candidates at what is known as the lowest unit charge. This is the sales rate for commercials that is charged to the station's regular high-volume advertisers. Broadcasters give discounts to advertisers who agree to buy many commercials over a long period of time. Politicians, however, buy a limited number of commercials over a short duration. Even so, the lowest-unit-charge provision of Section 315 forces broadcasters to sell political ads at the discounted price in order to keep broadcasters from making a financial windfall during election season.

Section 315 applies to all commercial and entertainment programming. Thus, California television stations could not run Arnold Schwarzenegger movies during his political campaign without triggering the equal opportunity rule for his opponent. This was the case during Ronald Reagan's campaigns as well. Legitimate newscasts, news interviews, and news documentary programs are exempt from Section 315, thus allowing journalistic freedom and discretion to escape the government's regulation of political broadcasting.

Congress added another layer of government oversight of the political campaign world in 2002 with the Bipartisan Campaign Reform Act, more commonly known as the McCain-Feingold Act. The law has many provisions regarding money and politics, but a key provision is to prevent organizations from spending money on broadcast ads that could be viewed as supporting a particular candidate within sixty days of a federal election. The law was challenged in the courts, but the Supreme Court, in a controversial 5–4 decision, upheld the law. Many First Amendment analysts and defenders, such as Nat Hentoff of the *Village Voice*, criticized the decision in that it restricts the voices of average citizens who pool resources in issue-oriented organizations.

The Supreme Court, however, apparently believes that the First Amendment can be used to negate overly restrictive campaign finance laws. A 2006 decision struck down a Vermont campaign finance law that placed a $300,000 spending limit on state gubernatorial campaigns and severely restricted individual campaign contributions. The Court's 6–3 majority said such low limits overly restricted the free speech rights of candidates to communicate with voters. It could also be said that the law restricted voters from speaking with their money to support the candidates they chose. This decision, along with the decision on McCain-Feingold, demonstrates the difficulty of courts trying to manage the role of the media and the expense of the media in political campaigns.

A particularly bad idea that keeps surfacing is the proposal to require broadcast stations to provide free airtime to political candidates. Former president Bill Clinton formally backed this notion in his 1998 State of the Union address. It showed up again in 2001 in a report by the National Commission on Federal Election Reform, led by former presidents Jimmy Carter and Gerald Ford. That commission recommended that TV broadcasters be required to provide presidential candidates five minutes of free airtime each night for the final thirty days of a campaign. Other proposals included providing such time for other officials. The premise is that broadcasters give something back to society in exchange for their broadcast licenses and that such free airtime would reduce the influence of money on politics.

This proposal is flawed in both practical and philosophical ways. First, giving candidates free time would surely not keep them from raising as much money as possible and then just using it for other things, likely paid political television time. Beyond that, average citizens would not sit still and watch these five-minute (or however long) epistles anyway. From a philosophical standpoint, the First Amendment should not allow the government to force supposed free speech broadcast outlets to communicate on certain subjects for certain amounts of time without a compelling interest. Clearly, political candidates have many avenues through which to disseminate their messages without forced access to broadcast airwaves.

Another ridiculous proposal being floated today, in mostly liberal circles, is to reinstate the Fairness Doctrine. The Fairness Doctrine was enforced as a rule of the Federal Communications Commission (FCC) from 1949 until the FCC abolished it in 1987. The doctrine mandated that broadcasters provide balanced coverage of controversial public issues. This, of course, put the government in the position of being able to second-guess broadcasters as to what constituted balance and what was considered to be a controversial public issue in the first place. The First Amendment implications of this doctrine were serious. How could broadcasters have free expression rights if the minute they expressed a point of view they had to turn around and provide a countering argument against themselves? How could free speech principles be served when the government was in a position to decide for broadcast journalists what was "fair"? The doctrine ultimately failed to accomplish its goal of fairness in that it chilled the atmosphere for public discussion, and most broadcasters refrained from engaging controversial issues at all for fear of lawsuits and possible FCC meddling. Instead of providing any fairness in public dialogue, the doctrine served to diminish discussion of public controversies altogether. Thus, the Reagan FCC dumped the Fairness Doctrine in 1987.

Since that time, mostly Democrats and liberal activists have argued to have the Fairness Doctrine reinstated. Until now, their legislative and legal battles have not been successful. Activists on the Left generally support the Fairness Doctrine because they believe its restoration and enforcement would choke off the many conservative commentators who have successfully taken over the radio airwaves. Under a Fairness Doctrine, a radio station that would program three hours of conservative commentator Sean Hannity would have to balance those three hours with commentary from somebody who had alternative views. Odds are the legislative efforts to get the Fairness Doctrine into law will not be successful until the Democrats control both houses of Congress and the White House. Then, the Supreme Court would soon thereafter likely strike the doctrine down on First Amendment grounds. Those who want "fairness" in the media marketplace, instead of pushing for legal remedies, should devote their energies more toward the marketplace of ideas and hope the ideas get traction with audiences. Broadcasters will surely find plenty of airtime for ideas that are valued by a sizable audience.

The media clearly play a key role in how politics is played in our nation. Citizens wanting to be fully informed about candidates and issues are well advised to gather their political information from a variety of credible sources. Citizens should also inoculate themselves as best as possible from the harsh rhetoric, misdirection, and emotional appeals of pundits and candidates. Doing so will allow voters to make rational, informed decisions that our political process sorely needs.

In 1959, Senator John Kennedy of Massachusetts wrote an article for *TV Guide* in which he warned of the potential harm the mass media could impose on the political process. He feared that politics could be taken over by "public relations experts" and challenged citizens to "perceive deception, to shut off gimmickry, to reward honesty, to demand legislation where needed." He asserted that the media's potential harm to the political process could happen only if the public acquiesced. Now, nearly fifty years later, Kennedy's warnings ring more profoundly than ever. It is up to the collective citizenry to "perceive deception" and "shut off gimmickry," or surely, we voters will see more and more of it.

# CHAPTER SEVEN

☞

# Media-Saturated Kids

It doesn't take a child psychologist, a media analyst, or an education researcher to figure out that television's overall effect on kids is negative. It only takes the commonest of sense to figure it out. Too many kids are not in good physical condition. They would be in better health if they did even moderate activity in place of the countless hours they spend watching television. Too many kids are exposed to crass and violent behaviors and foul language through the media and have those antisocial activities legitimized through the mediated examples they see. Too many kids are caught up in gross commercialization, no doubt influenced through "needs" created through the consumer culture of advertising. Too many kids have limited attention spans and need to be dazzled before they will focus on anything. School, church services, or even a family conversation are boring compared to the flashing lights, noise, and quick video edits of youth television programs.

None of this is to claim that television is the root of all youth problems. Certainly, there are many influences in society that contribute to making many kids overweight, inactive, bored, antisocial, and consumption driven. Weak parenting, the influence of peers, a lethargic educational system, and the general loss of cultural standards all contribute to the problems kids face. Those experts who think that kids would be fixed if suddenly they didn't watch television are surely misguided. They falsely hope that a complex problem can be addressed by a simple solution. A lot of very fine kids grow up and can overcome the negative influences of television and maybe even benefit from the sensible use of the media.

Television is just one of multiple factors affecting kids; however, it clearly is a major influence for many young people. Further, it is an influence that, if managed more effectively, could be moderated for the negative influences and even utilized for the potential positive influences. Sadly, effective management of kids' media usage is just not happening. The key reason for that, of course, is that parents don't effectively manage their own television habits, allowing the television to become an omnipresent influence in the home. Too often, parents are willing to let television content wash over the family, with television playing a role in virtually every waking moment of a family's day. The television is on during meals. Televisions are located throughout the house, including kids' rooms, basements, and other such places where parents can't keep track of what their children are seeing. The average home now has three or more working televisions. Even a ride in the car is a DVD event. Many parents are unwilling to restrict their own viewing in order to keep their kids from being exposed to inappropriate language, sex, and violence. Role modeling by parents of overuse and misuse of television is a major factor in developing kids who overuse and misuse television. Too many parents have either given up or don't see the need to manage their kids' television habits, much less their own.

Television is just one of many mediated influences on kids. Add video games, DVDs, and the Internet to this media gluttony. It can hardly be surprising that the cultural vision and values of kids are influenced by the various media inputs as much as, or more than, by the parents, churches, or schools. Reducing the role of media in the development and socialization of children won't be easy, but it needs to be done. The alternative is to surrender the values and beliefs of future generations to the framing being conducted by advertisers, Hollywood producers, and pop culture celebrities.

# The Statistical State of Media
## and Kids . . . and Commentary

When critics complain about the overwhelming presence of mediated messages in the lives of children, they aren't just barking at the moon. Beyond the anecdotal evidence and the evidence gathered from casual observation, numerous academic, educational, and think-tank studies provide a clear picture that a kid's lifestyle today is flooded hour by hour with electronic messages. Perhaps the media have become so much a part of kids' lives that parents (and kids) just take this deluge for granted. Everybody's kids have full access to television and computers, so it must be a good idea. Parents wanting to show their kids they care are eager to pamper their kids with the latest electronic gizmos, lest their kids feel slighted or left behind the neighbors. Kids feel entitled to have access to whatever shows their friends watch and on their own terms with regard to place and schedule. The research demonstrates how the media flood the lifestyles of children.

### Kids Spend Too Much Time in Front of Video Screens

A television is on somewhere in the American home about eight hours per day. Each person in the home watches television an average of about four hours per day. Even kids six years of age and younger watch television almost two hours per day, according to recent research by the Kaiser Family Foundation. Thirty-two percent of kids under six live in homes where the parents report that the television is on most of the time. Almost every American home now has two or more televisions and a fourth have four or more. Data from Nielsen Media Research show that the average American home has more televisions than people. Obviously, the kids are being washed over with television even when they aren't specifically watching a show. Add video games and computer use for some kids, and the total time spent with electronic influence is even higher. Evidence indicates that kids who view a lot of television have more difficulty reading at every grade level than kids who watch less television. There are indications that early and frequent television exposure can lead to attention deficit problems for children as young as seven. A *Los Angeles Times*/Bloomberg poll in 2006 found that over half of all teens multitasked with electronics while doing school homework, and it's not just casually listening to music while studying. Teens are watching television, movies, browsing the Internet, and instant messaging while trying to study.

*Comment*—Too much of anything can be harmful at a certain point. Even if the television is constantly tuned to socially beneficial programming, which it is surely not, too much television is disruptive to the normal development of kids. It's not that the television itself is so harmful. Some television can serve a sensible purpose and even be educational. A major problem with so much television exposure is the rhetorical message that parents send to children: television is an integral part of a family's existence. The ridiculous levels of electronic-screen consumption just serve to diminish the child's quality of life for all nonelectronic experiences. Kids who struggle to read need to watch less television. Kids who can't read well will struggle in many areas of school, employment, and life, while there is no upside for the kids who are great at watching the tube. Psychologists worry that teens doing electronic multitasking while doing homework absorb less of the educational material and might even be stunting brain development. Television, while having its uses in moderation, can't provide children the well-rounded life experiences that come with reading, being outdoors, having a family conversation, and so forth. Television becomes the easy diversion for kids and parents alike. And it's not just at home that kids have an overabundance of screen time. Ask your child how often they watch videos while at school. Teachers routinely show videos or allow students to play computer games at school. Sure, some of these videos are instructional, but even those essentially tell the kids that video screens are where the action is. Other videos shown at school are to fill time or to reward kids for something. Adults need to acknowledge that too much television is not helpful and work to develop alternate family or school activities that are beneficial for the kids. In particular, kids with attention deficit difficulties need to have tube time moderated, as pediatricians recommend. This takes effort and planning by parents, but the kids need it and deserve it. Many parents acknowledge that their families watch too much television, but they don't have the determination or guts to do anything about it.

## Kids Don't Need Televisions in Their Bedrooms

Various studies report that many kids have televisions in their own bedrooms. The Kaiser Foundation report found that 43 percent of kids aged four to six had televisions in their bedrooms, and 19 percent of kids under two had televisions in their bedrooms. Another study reported that almost two-thirds of kids aged eight to seventeen had televisions in their bedrooms. Not surprisingly, kids with televisions in their rooms watch an average of thirty minutes more television each day than kids who don't have televisions in their rooms. Sadly, the number one reason parents give for putting a TV in a child's room is so that the child is out of the way while the parents watch their own programs.

*Comment*—It's no wonder kids watch too much television. They have such easy access to it and it becomes part of their daily lifestyle. Kids can watch TV when they are getting dressed in the morning, when they are getting ready for bed, or when they are just hanging out in their rooms. With the television as a readily available source of diversion, why would a kid pick up a book? (That is, assuming there might be books in kids' bedrooms.) Of course, when the child watches television while holed up in his room, the opportunity for parents to supervise, comment on, or even know what is being watched is virtually nonexistent. Nearly a fourth of school-aged kids with televisions in their rooms report that the TV is on while they are trying to do their homework. Obviously, that can't be good for academic performance. Parents might think they are helping their kids by placing televisions in the kids' bedrooms, but this sort of overindulgence is absolutely counterproductive to developing healthy family television habits. Do the kid a favor and sell his or her television at the next garage sale. Kids can watch television in a family setting or not at all. Make the child do all computer use or video game play in a family area as well. This is not stifling or denying the child. Instead, it frees them from the tentacles of the screen. As for the parents who put TVs in their kid's room just so they can watch their own programs, shame on them for being so selfish and inconsiderate of the needs of their own child. This amounts to soft child abuse.

## Television Is Used in Some Really Stupid Ways

Parents report that they use television to reward their children for good behavior. The television is used as a babysitter to keep kids occupied while the parents do something they want to do. Forty percent of American families report that they normally watch television during dinner. The Kaiser study reported that 30 percent of parents of little kids use the television to help their kids fall asleep!

Comment—It is quite ridiculous that parents would use an electronic device with flashing bright lights and noise to help a child go to sleep. This is a clear sign of how irrational parents can be when it comes to managing the television habits of children. Whatever happened to the bedtime story; a good-night lullaby; and a dark, still room? All of the above "uses" of television demonstrate that parents have no common sense when it comes to television and their kids. Using television as a reward gives the kid the message that television is a wonderful thing that is worth their effort to acquire. Although not all television is of bad quality, enough of it is of poor quality and surely should not be considered a reward. What parent would give something potentially harmful to kids as a reward? That's essentially what happens when TV is a child's reward. "Hey kids, next time you behave as expected, your 'reward' is that you can ride in the car without a seatbelt or play in traffic." Dinnertime used to be a sacred time for families to talk to each other and get caught up on the day's events. A television blaring across the meatloaf makes that all but impossible. The hectic American lifestyle today leaves too little time to connect and really interact. Putting a television into the dinner hour makes such connection time almost impossible to achieve. As for using the television as a babysitter for while adults do other things, well, that's likely done even by the best of parents. But it should be a seldom-used strategy, and the "other things" need to be pretty darned important if the interests of the child are to be sacrificed during that time. A mother interviewed as part of the Kaiser research admitted she was willing to sacrifice her children's future for the short-term benefits of using a TV babysitter: "It makes life easier now, but in the long run, when they're older and starting to run into all these problems, I think I'll wish I wouldn't have let them do it [watch so much TV] when they were five." It's time for parents to wise up and muscle up.

## Kids Will Follow the Television Leads of Their Parents

In homes where the parents are characterized as heavy users of television, the kids will also become heavy users of television. Kids in such homes watch an average of over thirty minutes more television per day than kids in homes where parents are moderate viewers. Studies show that barely half of all homes have enforced rules about how much time a kid is allowed to watch television.

*Comment*—It doesn't take a genius to figure this out. Kids observe their parents' behavior and model it accordingly. That's true for many aspects of behavior and television use is no different. For one thing, if the adult is watching television a lot and the kid wants to be with the parent, he will just automatically be in the room with the television, absorbing whatever content the adult is viewing. Further, a parent who watches television a lot legitimizes television gluttony as a good use of one's time. The parent's lifestyle becomes the child's lifestyle. How can it be otherwise? Thus, when parents complain that their kids don't do well enough in school, are overweight, have few productive interests, and so forth, the parents must shoulder much of the blame for creating an environment that enables such patterns. Most parents strive to provide the best circumstances for their children to grow up. When it comes to television, video games, and so forth, parents allow their own weakness to be passed down to their kids. The lack of television rules in so many homes is a signal to the kids in those homes that any amount of viewing is okay and that there is no need to self-regulate or make program choices with care.

## Kids Are Exposed to Way Too Many Commercial Messages

The average child in America will view over forty thousand television commercials each year. The activist group TV-Turnoff Network reports that children as young as two have developed brand loyalty for certain products and that 97 percent of children under six have products based on characters from television shows.

*Comment*—Clearly, television is a powerful medium for commercial purposes and kids are influenced by advertising as much as or more than anybody else. Advertisers aren't pouring billions of dollars into commercials for children's programs as a public service. Advertisers know that children are vulnerable to commercial messages and that the preferences of kids ultimately influence the parents' buying decisions. The entire strategy of broadcast advertising is based on message repetition. That's why commercials aimed at children are run over and over. Kids can easily pick up the "television truth" that consumerism is important, that desiring material objects is expected, that certain foods are exciting and fun regardless of the nutritional value. Commercials aimed at kids aren't generally for products or foods that benefit kids or their parents. You just don't see commercials for broccoli. As one would expect, children who watch a lot of television are misguided when it comes to understanding nutrition. Media researcher Kristen Harrison of the University of Illinois studied the nutritional awareness of children in first through third grade. She found that the more television kids watch, the more confused they are about which foods are healthy and the less able they are to explain their food choices from a nutrition standpoint. Parents who are disturbed by their children's demands for new toys, unhealthy foods, and so on can diminish this focus by a reduction in the time their children watch television, particularly commercial television. Studies confirm that reducing the amount of a child's television viewing will reduce the influence of advertising on that child. The child won't harp and whine to purchase products that they haven't seen bombarded at them through glitzy marketing. This is plenty easy enough to figure out. Parents who tire of their kids' constant requests to purchase toys or candy (which is likely to be all parents) can effectively diminish that pattern by reducing the time their kids spend in front of a television.

The harm to kids from advertising is such that the American Academy of Pediatrics issued a policy statement on the matter in December 2006. The Academy statement details advertising's negative effects on kids, including obesity and other eating disorders, underage alcohol consumption, and engaging in sexual activity while too young. The Academy asked Congress and federal agencies to restrict junk food ads geared for young children and to more closely regulate the content of commercials dealing with alcohol and sexually related products like erectile dysfunction drugs. Certainly, inappropriate advertising targeted at kids is a national health issue in the eyes of the Academy.

## Television Exposes Kids to Antisocial Influences

The TV-Turnoff Network website provides some startling data regarding the amount of violence children see on television. The average American child will see about sixteen thousand televised murders before she or he reaches the age of eighteen. The child will see about two hundred thousand other violent acts on television by his or her eighteenth birthday. Ninety-one percent of children report that they are frightened by the violence they see on television. Beyond the physical violence that is so often portrayed, children are exposed to countless incidents of verbal violence. This violence includes harsh insults, shouted threats, mean-spirited criticism, belittling, and so forth. Media researcher Jim Potter asserts that this kind of verbal aggression frequently comes into our living rooms "flying under the radar" in that it is not as readily identified as violence. He asserts, however, that verbal violence may be just as frightening to children as violent acts. Kids in front of prime-time shows, as they often are, see not only the violence, but the sexual suggestiveness, bathroom humor, and general rudeness. Even television targeted at kids includes plenty of questionable material. The Parents Television Council (PTC) monitored over four hundred hours of television targeted at kids aged five to ten. The study found over six violent incidents per hour, even after removing the "cartoony" violence of Wile E. Coyote and such. That amount of violence is higher than what is found per hour in prime time. The PTC also found plenty of verbal aggression (2 per hour), disruptive and disrespectful behavior (1.34 per hour), along with offensive and/or sexually suggestive comments (over 1 per hour) . . . and this is in programming for kids.

   *Comment*—Clearly, there are many influences on kids, good and bad, that make them turn out the way they do. Television is just one cultural influence. Many parents rationalize that they watched a lot of antisocial behavior on television while growing up, and they turned out just fine. Even if these parents really are properly adjusted and functioning adults, how do they know their child will not be affected negatively by absorbing countless mediated examples of violent acts, violent language, snotty behavior, bathroom jokes, and sexual language? They can't. Not to mention that television content, by all accounts, is more edgy today than a generation ago. Television is a legitimizer of behavior and cultural standards. Parents must ask themselves if the standards being portrayed on television are the ones they endorse and to what degree they want their kids exposed to those warped standards. Sure, parents can't completely immunize their children from the antisocial influences of the world, but television is surely not the best way to have kids gain their experience with the world's dim humor and reckless violence. The verbal violence, indeed, does fly under the radar, as many parents believe that kids' exposure to just words can't be that harmful. Interestingly, as Potter asserts, verbal violence monitored on television can be quite harmful because it is easier to imitate in real life than the more dramatic and physical forms of violence. It can hardly be a surprise that children who watch the most television are more likely to exhibit bullying behaviors on grade school playgrounds. They've seen this behavior modeled in the media and have fewer nonmediated experiences from which to draw examples of appropriate behavior. None of this discussion is to suggest that television is the cause of all child social problems, but ignoring the role of television is equally off base. In the modern era, kids do need some television in their lives. To eliminate television from the lifestyle of any child would surely make that youngster clueless regarding the mediated world and single him or her out as a nerd, detached from the kids who do watch television. The key is for parents to actually make choices about how much and what kinds of television the kids, newborn through high school, should be allowed to watch. Viewing needs to be done in moderation, consist of socially valuable shows, and be balanced with nonmediated experiences to round out a day. Virtually every bit of research confirms that kids who watch a lot of television have more social problems, are less physically fit, and perform more poorly in school. Does the television cause these things to happen or do kids with these difficulties just gravitate toward watching television? Who knows for sure? But common gumption dictates that the first step in helping our kids be socially adjusted, healthy, and better educated is to get them away from the electronic screen.

## Video Games Are Part of the Problem

Sure, playing an occasional video game based on football, golf, a maze, or something fun is no big deal. Spending too much time with video games, however, no matter how fun, leads to the same problems as watching too much television. The amount of time invested, along with the thematic content of the games, are the keys. Parents keeping track of total screen time for their kids need to combine television and video-game time. Kicking a child away from the television only to have him go play video games is ill-advised and ignores the cumulative effect of total screen time in replacing other, more productive activities.

The major concern about video games is the graphic and overly violent content of many games. For good reason, psychologists, educators, and media researchers worry about the effect of demented video games on the young people who play them, particularly those most vulnerable to the negative influences of viewing and acting out video game violence. As with researching all human behavior, proving linkages between video game use and changes of attitudes, not to mention behavior, is difficult. Still, it stands to reason that young people who thrill themselves for hours doing video games that focus on violence and committing crimes are not doing themselves any good.

The available research gives credibility to the concerns about violent video games. Researchers at the Indiana University School of Medicine have found that the brains of youths with high amounts of past video-violence exposure react to new exposures differently than youths with smaller amounts of prior exposure. Essentially, youths with previous high exposure to video violence generate less brain activity in the area of the brain responsible for making appropriate decisions. Worse yet, youths with previous behavior disorders had less brain activity in those critical areas of the brain while playing violent video games than adolescents without such behavior problems. Thus, it appears that susceptible youths with already defined behavior problems are affected more negatively by using violent video games.

Psychology researcher Bruce Bartholow at the University of Missouri has generated research that suggests frequent violent video game play leads to diminished brain function and desensitizes the players to real-world violence. This, of course, raises the prospect that more aggressive real-life behavior could be a spin-off of chronic violent video game play. This sort of research is ongoing and largely preliminary, but indications from these and other studies are that violent video game play is related to aggressive behavior. So parents, if your teenage son isn't aggressive enough already, be sure to get him plenty of video games to help him waste time in between his antisocial outbursts.

## A Television Channel Just for Babies?

Although most pediatricians and psychologists recommend that babies shouldn't watch any television, we now have a channel targeted directly at that young audience. BabyFirstTV made its debut in the spring of 2006 as a premium channel available through the DirecTV satellite system. BabyFirstTV hopes to eventually be included in cable packages around the country. The channel targets little kids from six months to three years of age. It is programmed around the clock each day, so a restless kid who can't sleep can watch television at all hours of the night! Thankfully, it doesn't include commercials, but it's probably just a matter of time until the characters and songs end up in toy stores or in BabyFirstTV catalogs.

Frankly, if kids under three are going to be in front of a television, BabyFirstTV might be as good as anything for them to watch. The assumption being made by this channel's very existence, however, is that television is an essential aspect of life even for the littlest of viewers. The BabyFirstTV website promotes its channel with the slogan "Watch your baby blossom." This parallel to a plant is apropos in that many parents will simply "plant" their baby in front of the channel and hope for something good to happen. The channel promotes the positive benefits of age-appropriate television, suggesting a linkage to "notable improvements in a toddler's spoken vocabulary." The channel trumpets the opportunity for "unique parent co-viewing experiences." But seriously folks, what are the odds of parents sitting still and watching these programs *with* their babies? Much more likely, of course, is that the parents will be doing other things on their own while the kid vegetates in front of the tube. Of course, if the parent really does have the time to sit with the kid during television viewing, that amount of time would be better spent with the parent engaging the child with talk, physical activity, reading, and anything more productive than screen time.

Other channels are getting into the act of targeting the littlest of viewers. Nickelodeon, the Disney Channel, Discovery Kids, and even PBS are all now designing programs intended for kids three years old and younger. If there are eyeballs and dollars to be had, television will do what it takes to get them, regardless of how exploitative of the youngest Americans it all might seem.

## The Government's Involvement in Managing Children's Television

The concern for how television impacts children is such that the nation's lawmakers have taken the unusual step to get involved in trying to manage the content of television programming. The Children's Television Act of 1990 (CTA) was passed by Congress as a wide-ranging attempt to bring some sense to the exploitive world of children's television. The FCC is empowered to manage and enforce the provisions of the act. Although most broadcasters and free speech advocates think government intrusion into media processes is a bad idea, nobody has wanted to risk the "anti-child" image damage that would come with fighting the matter in court.

Through the CTA, broadcasters are required to provide at least three hours each week of programs designed especially to meet the educational needs of children sixteen years of age and younger. Those programs must be at least thirty minutes in length and be regularly scheduled. Defining what counts as educational programming, however, is left to the broadcasters. The FCC has imposed limits on how much commercial time can be aired in children's programs. Children's programming on weekends is limited to 10.5 minutes of commercials per hour and programming on weekdays is limited to 12 minutes per hour. (Nobody really knows why kids can be allowed to see more commercials on weekdays compared to weekends.) Broadcasters are prohibited from airing commercials for toys or products based on characters within a particular show. Hosts of children's shows cannot do commercials within their own shows. Announcements must be made to notify children of the separation between the program content and the commercials. Interestingly, although the FCC generally stays away from regulating nonbroadcast television, these rules for children's television are applied to cable and satellite programmers.

The FCC has conducted spot audits of broadcast and cable outlets to verify adherence to the children's television rules. Violators have received hefty penalties. In a high-profile enforcement in 2004, the ABC Family Channel was fined $500,000 and Nickelodeon was fined a million dollars for airing too many commercials during kids' programs. In a statement announcing the fines, then FCC chairman Michael Powell said that children "are uniquely vulnerable as viewers" and warned broadcasters that the commission will "vigorously enforce our children's advertising limits."

The Telecommunications Act of 1996 included a provision that requires television manufacturers to include what is known as a V-chip, a technical device that allows parents to block programs they deem unsuitable for children. Also in 1996, Congress browbeat the television industry into creating a "voluntary" ratings system to label the age appropriateness for all shows. These initiatives, while well-intentioned, have been busts from an effectiveness standpoint. Less than 20 percent of parents have ever used V-chips to block programs from their kids . . . and who knows how many tech-savvy kids have unblocked the shows to watch them anyway. Most other parents don't know that V-chips exist in their TV sets or how to operate them. The ratings system has been equally ineffective. Most viewers have no idea what the letters, like FV (fantasy violence) or D (suggestive dialogue), stand for. The television industry has responded to this confusion by making the letters on the screen bigger. Further, the PTC has reported that the ratings are inconsistently applied both within and among networks. V-chips, of course, won't block programs that aren't labeled accurately in the first place.

Lawmakers aren't done with their efforts to shield children from the effects of the screen. Senators David Rockefeller of West Virginia and Kay Bailey Hutchison of Texas introduced legislation in 2005 to go after excessive violence on television. As their effort asserts, violent content might be as harmful as the indecent content that is already regulated. The legislation didn't get traction in 2005, but the issue won't go away soon and perhaps just needs the jumpstart of a high-profile incident to get it moving, much like the Super Bowl wardrobe malfunction served to get fines raised for broadcast indecency. Legislation has been proposed to confront violent and pornographic video games. Sponsored by Senators Hillary Clinton of New York, Evan Bayh of Indiana, and Joe Lieberman of Connecticut, the Family Entertainment Protection Act would prohibit businesses from selling mature-themed video games to anyone under the age of seventeen. A number of states have already passed laws to limit kids' access to dangerous video games, some of which are already being challenged in the courts.

A government task force to study the link between childhood obesity and too much media consumption was launched in the fall of 2006. Senator Sam Brownback of Kansas and FCC chairman Kevin Martin are two of the leaders of the effort. Neither has indicated that the task force will eventually recommend any legislation or government mandates to confront the problem, saying only that the media industry should address the problem while receiving guidance from the government task force. Some kids' advocates are hoping that television programmers will stop advertising junk foods and such during kids' television shows. Even if that happened, it's hard to imagine it would do much to alleviate childhood obesity and inactivity. Kids have to get away from the screen in order to be more active and fit. Don't wait for the television industry to start sending that message.

Sadly, however, laws to regulate the television/video culture ultimately do little good and come off largely as symbolic gestures. Even if kids do watch the few hours of socially relevant and educational programming required by law, the impact of those messages is likely overwhelmed by the countless hours of other shows they watch. V-chips are of no help if parents don't use them. Preventing retailers from selling violent video games directly to kids will surely not keep the kids from accessing these games through other avenues. Nobody should expect that legislation can ultimately protect kids from the damaging effects of the media. It will take a shift in cultural values.

## Parents Need to Establish Their Home's Media Culture

Parents can't directly control the many cultural influences that bombard their children while at school, the playground, and so forth. But the parents can control the manner in which the media are used in their own homes. Establish rules. Focus your kid's attention on the many acceptable programs available to watch. Don't prohibit television altogether, thus making your kid a nerd amongst his or her peers. Be aware of what content is being absorbed not only by your kid but also by other parents' kids. Your child need not watch poor programming to be influenced by the potty mouths and bullying of kids who are watching the wrong programs. Parents who have the courage to stand up to their own kids can effectively manage the media environments in their homes. The major concern for our society, however, is what happens to the kids whose parents don't effectively manage their media.

The concerns and potential for harm caused by kids' excessive exposure to television can't be overstated. Parents need to understand that the screen environment today is, indeed, more potentially harmful than when they grew up, both in content and the ease of access. Leading researchers Dimitri Christakis and Frederick Zimmerman wrote an editorial in 2006 in which they called childhood exposure to television and video games a major public health issue. They pointed out the links between heavy exposure to screen media and weight problems, aggressive behavior, early risky sex, and increased use of alcohol and tobacco. That pretty much defines a national public health problem. We all suffer from the consequences.

# CHAPTER EIGHT

〃

# Big Media, Little Responsibility

Since its inception, broadcasting in America was designed to serve local audiences. In the 1920s, Commerce Secretary Herbert Hoover devised a public interest standard that granted broadcast licenses to stations in specific, local communities and required those broadcasters to serve the public interests of those locales. For decades, radio and television stations were normally owned by people who lived in the communities where their stations operated. The Federal Communications Commission (FCC) was committed to keeping broadcasters locally focused by maintaining strict limits as to how many stations any one individual or corporation could own. Up until 1984, no single entity could own more than twenty-one total broadcast properties, and no more than seven in any one service (television, AM, or FM). The limits were designed to make sure that ownership of the American airwaves was spread around and not subject to domination by a handful of well-funded conglomerates. The theory was that more voices could get access to the media marketplace and that owners would be more committed to the communities in which their broadcast stations operated. The rule survived court challenges from opponents who said the restrictions were arbitrary.

It doesn't take a logic expert to figure that the closer a media owner is to the community, both geographically and emotionally, the more conscientious and committed that owner will be to understanding and serving that community. A crass bottom-line mentality prevails with distant corporate ownership of media properties in local communities, and "community service" is relegated only to those activities for which a profit can be made. This is not to say that making money cannot be the top priority for any media company. The American media system is totally based on capitalism. Media owners, individuals or corporations, should not be expected to lose money in providing broadcast or even newspaper services to a community. It also stands to reason, however, that a corporate board of directors in an East Coast high-rise building will define broadcasting success only in terms of quarterly bottom-line reports and will have little or no concern about the issues, values, and interests of any particular city in which it owns a media property.

Proponents of big media argue that ownership of media properties should be generally unregulated, provided monopolistic practices aren't going on. The marketplace, they argue, should determine who owns which media outlets and how many media properties an entity should be allowed to control. Owning media properties, however, is not like owning fast-food franchises or manufacturing widgets. Owning a media property brings with it a larger responsibility because the products being peddled are news, entertainment, culture, and the very identity of a society, both broadly defined and in terms of each locale. The commodity of a money-making media corporation is the very flow of ideas and information a democracy needs to exist and to function effectively. A society and its government have a tremendous duty to fully assess and manage who controls the media and to what effect. Broadcast properties operate on publicly owned airwaves. Thus, the government has an obligation to guarantee that those airwaves are used to serve the interests of the citizens, owners of those public airwaves. The government must assure that there is a marketplace of ideas and a sensible flow of relevant, local information. That is sufficient reason to carefully and deliberately measure the media ownership regulations for our nation. Instead, however, Congress and the FCC have bowed to the pressures of big media and the false promises of marketplace demands. The result has been a growing influence of a handful of big media corporations; displaced and distant ownership of broadcast properties; and the loss of local content, priorities, and values in American electronic media.

## The Telecommunications Act of 1996
## Opens the Floodgates

The era of deregulating the broadcast industry began during the Reagan administration and curiously continued unabated during the Democratic administration of Bill Clinton. To be sure, many moves to free the broadcasting industry from bureaucratic paperwork and cumbersome reports were long overdue. Eliminating the ineffective and theoretically void Fairness Doctrine, which didn't promote fairness and instead stifled discussion, was also a wise move. Removing government bureaucracy in reasonable amounts from the private business of broadcasting does have some benefit.

The removal of most ownership restrictions, however, is quite another matter from downsizing government paperwork requirements. In 1984, the FCC expanded ownership limits from seven AM stations, seven FM stations, and seven television stations to limits of twelve of each service. In the early 1990s, the commission raised ownership levels for radio stations, allowing any owner to have up to thirty of each, AM and FM. This deregulation momentum really took off when Congress passed and President Clinton signed the Telecommunications Act of 1996. Proponents of the deregulation argued that there were now so many media outlets and other avenues of mass communication available to society that the government could relax its ownership rules and society would still have a wide range of diverse voices to provide news, commentary, and entertainment.

Among other things, the act lifted all limits on how many radio stations an entity could own nationwide and raised the number of stations an owner could have in any one market. It allowed an owner to operate multiple radio and television stations in the same market. It provided for television owners to buy stations in as many markets as possible up to a reach of 35 percent of the national audience. It also extended terms of broadcast licenses for radio and television stations to eight years, meaning stations had longer periods in between license renewals, when each station must justify its license to the FCC. And with an eye to even further loosening of ownership rules, Congress mandated that the FCC revisit the limits every two years and to modify any regulation found to no longer be in the public interest. That was code, of course, for relaxing the ownership limits even further and giving big media corporations even more power over the nation's broadcast enterprise.

The effects of these relaxed rules were immediate and profound as large corporations took advantage of the new rules to buy out smaller owners and expand influence. Corporate radio giant Clear Channel went on a buying spree and now owns over twelve hundred radio stations, over 10 percent of the commercial stations in the country. Within five years of the act, the total number of radio owners dropped by over 25 percent as big media corporations bought out their smaller competitors, thus reducing the number of separate media voices nationally and within many communities. Within seven years, the number of radio owners nationally had dropped by 35 percent. The same thing happened in television, where the big corporations owning networks went on buying sprees to add to their local market properties, again reducing the number of smaller broadcast owners. In no time, big broadcasters were up against the 35 percent national coverage limit and were at the FCC asking for exemptions to go beyond that limit.

The major philosophic effect of congressional and FCC relaxation of broadcast ownership rules is that the government abandoned its long-held position that the public benefits from having the many, diverse, and local voices that come with a commitment to spreading broadcast properties around. Once the government caved to the lobbying of corporate media giants and declared that market forces and big media could sufficiently determine and effectively meet the information and cultural needs of American communities, the rationale for imposing any limits at all went down the drain. Without a commitment to localism in ownership and without the rationale that many different mediated voices best serve the dialogue needs of a democracy, the FCC was in no position to defend media ownership restrictions of any sort.

## Regulatory Paralysis Ensues

A Three Stooges movie looks like a model of rational behavior compared to what has happened at the FCC and in the courts lately, as the impossible task of balancing public interest and ownership limits moves forward. The FCC's congressionally mandated review of ownership limits in 2000 concluded that no adjustments to the 1996 Telecommunications Act were needed. Fox television and other media giants wanting to own more outlets battled the FCC decision at the District of Columbia (DC) Circuit Court. That court criticized the FCC for its "arbitrary and capricious" decision on keeping ownership levels as they were, and ordered the FCC back to the drawing board to either further loosen ownership rules or somehow make a case for why not.

The FCC commissioners were unable to find anything near a consensus. The three Republican commissioners, led by Chairman Michael Powell, outvoted the other two commissioners in 2003 and issued new rules to raise the television ownership cap to 45 percent of national coverage, allow TV duopolies in most markets, raise ownership limits for individual radio markets, and even allow cross-ownership of broadcast and newspaper outlets in the same communities. If the DC court wanted loosened ownership restrictions, the FCC was ready to oblige. The FCC report tried to show the DC court that the traditional public interest objectives of competition, diversity of voices, and localism could all be supported even while media giants asserted more control over the media landscape. The FCC even calculated a Diversity Index Methodology to support its claims. But even Moe, Curly, and Larry can infer, all statistics aside, that competition, diversity, and localism automatically diminish when big, absent corporate owners get fatter.

Predictably, forces opposed to letting big media bully the FCC sprinted to court to stop the new rules from taking effect. The Prometheus Radio Project, a grassroots media interest, led the charge and took the legal challenge to a more friendly venue, the Third Circuit Court of Appeals in Philadelphia. That court, though divided, gave the antideregulatory challengers a victory and stopped the FCC's proposed rules that would have allowed further growth of big media. The Third Circuit judges were unimpressed by the FCC's Diversity Index Methodology, saying the statistical gymnastics asked them to "abandon both logic and reality." No kidding. By the FCC's calculation, a New York community college TV station was credited with making the same contribution to viewpoint diversity as the *New York*

*Times* and its co-owned radio station. Other assertions in the Diversity Index Methodology were just as far-fetched.

Regulatory paralysis has now set in. The FCC is now working against two court setbacks, one seeking justification from the FCC on why ownership limits shouldn't be increased and one slamming the FCC for its feeble rationale for supporting such increases. Having apparently abandoned its philosophic commitment to providing multiple broadcast voices and supporting localism, the FCC is left rudderless and with virtually no argumentative ammunition. As he was heading out the door as FCC chairman, Michael Powell called the recent legal decisions "chaotic" and said the state of media law is now "clouded and confused." He has that right.

In an incredible irony, while the FCC was a leading conspirator in loosening ownership regulations, the commission went around the country wringing its hands and holding public hearings on . . . how to best maintain localism in American broadcasting.

## "Big Media" Really Are Big

A relative handful of big media corporations dominate American media services and play a large role in determining how citizens are entertained and informed. They also define cultural values and fuel the advertising world. While Americans are generally skeptical of big oil, big merchandisers like Wal-Mart, big banks, big auto manufacturers, and so on, most are oblivious to the magnitude of the major media corporations. A quick review of some media giants gives us an indication of their breadth and potential economic and cultural influence.

- TimeWarner is the largest media corporation in the world. It owns multiple television and cable networks, the second largest cable distribution system in the country, and over a hundred magazines. It also owns movie production companies and a number of Internet services.
- Walt Disney owns multiple movie and video production companies, television networks, cable channels, dozens of radio stations, a number of local television stations, book publishers, and, of course, theme parks.

- News Corp is international in scope but has a large footprint in the United States. It owns a television network and several cable networks. It owns multiple television stations, covering more of the United States than any other single television owner. It owns film production companies, a satellite TV distribution system, newspapers, magazines, a radio network, and book publishers . . . to say nothing of its international holdings in Australia and Europe.
- NBC Universal is a subsidiary of megacorporation General Electric. It owns more local television stations than any other single owner in the country. It owns the Spanish-language Telemundo network, along with NBC Universal Television Studios and eight cable television channels. It owns Universal Pictures and Universal Parks and Resorts, among other various entities.
- CBS owns two broadcast networks, a book publishing company, a radio network, and dozens of radio and television stations.
- Clear Channel owns about twelve hundred radio stations, a huge outdoor advertising operation, fourteen television stations (and manages twenty-seven others for largely absent owners), and the nation's largest concert promotion operation.

A major problem is not just that these corporations are so big and control so much media stuff, but that they are "vertically integrated"; in other words, they control messages from development through delivery. For example, companies that produce content can see that their material is delivered through their own media outlets. An operation like Clear Channel can easily impact the music world by managing which artists get airtime on its many radio stations *and* managing which artists get traction in its concert venues around the country. The horizontal integration allows big companies like TimeWarner to gain a wide influence on Americans through broadcast media, cable distribution, and print circulation. News Corp impacts society through its over-the-air network and local stations; and through its cable channels; and through its movie productions; and through its print resources like newspapers, magazines, and books. It's unlikely any media-consuming American has escaped the influence of multiple inputs from the big corporations like Clear Channel, TimeWarner, News Corp, and the others. Media innovator Ted Turner recently wrote of the dangers of big media corporations controlling the production studios, the broadcast outlets, the cable outlets, and Internet sites. He wrote, "Big media today wants to own the faucet, pipeline, water, and the reservoir. The rain clouds come next."

Having big corporations get bigger is pretty much the way of American capitalism, and there is virtually nothing the government can or should do in terms of regulating networks, print publishing, movie production, and even the Internet. But when it comes to regulating who owns publicly owned airwaves, the government does have a reason and a responsibility to get involved. The Congress has legislated and the courts have upheld the public interest standard in regulating ownership of individual radio and television stations. The government has a right, even an obligation, to make sure that radio and television airwaves are managed in a way that serves the "public interest, convenience, and necessity." In this regard, it can be argued that local audiences are better served when ownership of local stations is not dominated by distant mammoth corporations.

## News Coverage Is Generally More Extensive with Smaller Ownership

Localism in media ownership is most critically important when it comes to providing news to the citizens of a region. It has been said that the media serve a surrogate role for the public. In no case is this more important than when it comes to delivering local information to citizens about their political leaders, the area's economy, the region's educational progress, social standards, and countless other matters that confront residents each day. Without this vital information, citizens cannot effectively monitor their civic leaders and effect change to assure that those leaders are serving the public will. It has been said that news is the conversation of democracy. That claim applies on both the national and local levels. If local news is ineffectively provided, it only stands to reason that the democratic functioning of a geographic area will not be as effective as it should be. The major question is whether distant big media ownership, with a bottom line–only mentality, can find within itself the commitment and dedication to any geographic area to spend the resources needed to adequately inform the citizenry. Big corporations are happy to deliver the ears and eyeballs of citizens to advertisers for the financial gain of both the media corporations and the advertisers. Sadly, as emerging studies are now indicating, these corporations are not as willing to devote their resources in the proper proportion to see that their audiences are informed about matters that serve the "public interest, convenience, and necessity."

One study that seems to support the conclusion that local broadcast ownership results in more news programming that is decidedly local comes from, of all places, the FCC. The FCC, which has worked hard in recent years to remove ownership restrictions in an apparent appeasement of giant media corporations, prepared a study in 2004 to look at how ownership structures impacted local broadcast news. The study only came to light in 2006 when Senator Barbara Boxer asked about it during the reconfirmation hearing of FCC commissioner Kevin Martin. Martin indicated he didn't know anything about the report, and the reasons for the mysterious hiding of the report have not been made clear. The report's conclusions, however, could well indicate why the deregulatory FCC would not be happy to have the report distributed. The report clearly asserts that local audiences are better served from a broadcast news standpoint when the broadcast owners are local.

The FCC report categorized and measured the content of broadcast newscasts and then compared its findings with ownership characteristics. The study indicated that locally owned television stations air significantly more local news than stations owned by broadcast networks or stations owned by nonlocal corporations. It is difficult to state exactly why local ownership appears to promote more local news coverage, but the report raises some plausible explanations. One is that a local owner is in a better position to monitor the news coverage and doesn't rely on other layers of administration for that monitoring. Another is that the owner's own local interests and involvements in the community help serve the drive for more local news. What might be working is just the simple logic that an owner with headquarters in a particular community is naturally going to be more aware of what is happening in that community and more concerned for the welfare of that community and its citizens.

Another study also suggests a relationship between ownership and overall local news quality. A 2003 study by the Project for Excellence in Journalism suggested that television stations owned by smaller ownership groups produced higher quality newscasts than stations owned by larger corporations. It also found that stations merely affiliated with networks produced higher quality newscasts than stations owned by networks. Local ownership, however, did not necessarily create better newscasts. The study evaluated dozens of newscasts from markets around the country. It defined quality in terms of various characteristics like fairness, balance, community focus, enterprise, and significance. The report indicates the complexity of connecting ownership factors to newscast quality, but asserts that large corporate ownership could well diminish the quality of local news content.

Studies like these, and others, have gotten the attention of lawmakers, who question whether increased media consolidation ultimately diminishes service to local news audiences. Senator John McCain of Arizona bashed broadcasters after release of a report from the Lear Center of the University of Southern California. That report showed a troubling lack of political coverage by television stations during the 2004 election season. It showed that just 8 percent of newscasts studied in a national examination contained any coverage of a local political race. McCain has argued that absence of local campaign coverage is connected to consolidation of ownership in the media industry. At a press conference in 2005, McCain complained that broadcasters were more likely to cover accidents than local political campaigns: "From what I gather, if a local candidate wants to be on television, and cannot afford to advertise, his only hope may be to have a freak accident." McCain introduced to the Senate a bill titled "Localism in Broadcasting Reform Act of 2005." The bill was designed to shorten license terms for broadcasters and more fully require stations to demonstrate to the FCC how they were serving the local audience. The bill got no traction before Congress adjourned, but congressional leaders like McCain are clearly concerned about ownership, localism, and news coverage, and they are unlikely to let the issue drift away.

## Big Media Ownership Linked to Indecent Content on Airwaves?

If a big corporation located a continent away owns a radio station in your community, what are the odds that the absentee corporate executives know what's going on at that station or have much sense about the community's cultural standards? Likely, it's a long shot. Although drawing a direct cause-and-effect relationship might be difficult, evidence compiled by the Center for Creative Voices indicates a link between big media ownership and the amount of indecent content emanating from their broadcast properties. A study released in 2005 showed that the four largest radio ownership groups (Clear Channel, Viacom, Entercom, and Emmis), with a 48 percent share of the national audience, accounted for 96 percent of all FCC-imposed fines for indecency violations. The report found that as local stations were gobbled up by big media companies, the new owners were prone to replace locally produced content with edgier fare produced in distant markets. The buying spree of locally owned stations, of course, was prompted in 1996 when ownership levels were radically loosened.

FCC commissioner Michael Copps responded to the report by saying it only made sense that attention to community standards drifts away when control of local broadcasting moves away to large and removed media conglomerates. Copps has been a consistent voice at the commission in calling for a deliberate approach to changes in ownership rules, fearing that the loss of localism reduces the ability of broadcasters to serve the public interest.

## Other Content Concerns Raised by Ownership Consolidation

It is quite difficult to fully assess the many influences brought on to our society by the continued growth of big media. One thing is certain, however—big media operations are sure to affect not only the ownership and regulatory landscape, but ultimately what messages audiences receive.

## Fewer Companies Now Produce Prime-Time Television Shows

In the early 1990s, the major networks owned less than 15 percent of all prime-time programs aired on those networks. Independent producers created and produced the wide majority of such programs. Now, thanks to relaxed federal regulation and the growth of media conglomerates, over three-fourths of all prime-time network programming is owned by the networks. The big networks own the production companies, the content, and the distribution avenues of the prime-time programs. Independent producers had better come up with something really good or try to sell their programs to fringe cable channels. Networks are hardly going to give the independent producers a fair shot to access the prime-time audience because of the finances involved. Networks make the most money by putting their own productions on the air, promoting them, building an audience, and then making even more money when they peddle the programs into syndication.

## Payola Temptations Associated with Big Radio Corporations

It should come as no surprise that four of the largest radio corporations have come under FCC suspicion for "payola," the practice of providing radio personnel with cash or gifts in exchange for playing and promoting certain songs on the radio. Rules against the practice have been in place since the celebrated payola hearings of 1960. In April 2006, the FCC sent letters of inquiry, the first step of an investigation that could lead to fines for radio giants Clear Channel, CBS, Entercom Communications, and Citadel Broadcasting. When a handful of big radio corporations control so many radio stations, it must be quite tempting for the music industry to seek to buy influence into those many stations to get certain songs or artists promoted. This FCC inquiry comes on the heels of a settlement in 2005 between New York attorney general Eliot Spitzer and Warner Music Group, a part of another media conglomerate, after a lengthy pay-for-play investigation. Published reports have indicated that Spitzer is not finished with his payola investigations and is now targeting radio corporations for their roles. The FCC inquiry, it appears, might have been sparked, in part, by Spitzer's sharing of information with the FCC. Clearly, this kind of bribery investigation takes a good deal of time to ferret out, but just as clearly, the investigation is looking at the radio and music industries at the highest corporate levels.

## Media Concentration Hurts Kids' Television?

FCC commissioner Michael Copps has suggested that media consolidation has hurt the amount and quality of programming directed at children. Speaking in 2006 to a children's activist conference, Copps pointed to data being collected by an organization called Children Now, saying the data indicate a deterioration of children's programming in certain markets and bear additional study by the FCC as it reviews ownership and consolidation rules.

## Generic, Formulaic, and Vanilla Programming for Radio Listeners

Although most radio listeners are unaware, it's quite likely the air personalities you hear on your hometown radio stations are not physically present in your community. Many stations are now remotely programmed from a radio corporation's home office, with the programs being delivered via satellite to stations around the country. The local radio station is local only in the sense that the transmitter tower is in your community and a few local sales executives see to it that commercials are broadcast for local businesses. Your local pop music station or country station is likely playing the same songs in the same order as dozens of other stations around the country. Although there are exceptions, truly local radio personalities are disappearing. The announcers in remote locations will try gimmicks to make you think they know your community. In preprogrammed comments, they'll comment about a local ball team or roadway, or check a remote weather radar screen and talk about the rain in the area. They might even mention request lines that are generally ignored. But if you drop by the station's office, you won't find your favorite deejay on the premises. Regional differences for most radio formats have disappeared.

Radio's number one strength, immediacy, has also disappeared. The satellite-delivered or voice-tracked programs are produced hours in advance of when they might be aired and thus cannot respond to breaking events. Except for a possible news-talk station in a community, odds are the other radio stations carry no newscasts at all. This is not only bad radio but it fails to serve the public interest and could even be dangerous for a community. In 2002, a train derailment in Minot, North Dakota, released a chemical cloud over the city. Police began calling the six commercial radio stations to seek help in getting the emergency information out to the community. All six commercial stations in Minot are owned by Clear Channel, headquartered in San Antonio, Texas. Police were unable to reach anyone at the stations and there was a lengthy delay until radio personnel could be reached at home and the emergency broadcasts aired. Clear Channel later said that a staffer was on duty at the time, but jammed phone lines prevented the police call from getting through. There were other technical problems that prevented the emergency messages from being broadcast directly from the police. There was enough blame to go around, but surely, the situation was complicated because the radio stations in Minot were being remotely programmed and the local staff presence was minimal.

Musicians have complained to the FCC about mega radio corporations, saying that it is difficult to get airplay when music playlists are determined at the national level. New and local musical groups can't get traction when local stations are programmed from corporate headquarters hundreds of miles away. The musical community says this closes the market for creative new talent and leaves the music industry to recycle already established groups and sounds.

Radio licenses are awarded by the FCC to owners who promise to serve the public interests of the community to which the license is awarded. Federal regulators make a serious mistake when they award licenses to owners who provide no distinctly local service.

## Cross-Ownership Diminishes Voices in Communities

For years, owners of broadcast properties have been prohibited from owning a newspaper in the same market, except for a few unusual or grandfathered situations. The theory was that more journalistic competition was beneficial to the public and that having more owners in a community allowed more perspectives and voices to be heard. The FCC tried to eliminate this rule in 2003, basing its decision on the rapidly expanding media landscape and the deteriorating financial picture of the newspaper industry. Proponents of broadcast-print cross-ownership argued that the public would see an increase in local news output and quality because the single owner could reduce duplicative costs of newsgathering and distribute its news service across multiple platforms. The Third Circuit Court of Appeals, however, overturned the FCC decision and kept the cross-ownership prohibition in place, saying the FCC had not fully justified the change in direction. The FCC has gone back to the drawing board to reconsider its overall ownership rules, and a key matter for debate is whether owners of broadcast properties should also own print media outlets in the same community. One thing is obvious, however—the more media properties owned by any one entity in a community, the fewer voices there are to fuel the conversation of democracy and to compete in establishing a community's news agenda. Even in a large market like Los Angeles or New York, one entity owning the major daily newspaper and a highly rated television station exerts a large influence on a community's media business and flow of information, regardless of how many other "little voices" are in the mix.

## The FCC Needs to Go Very Slowly in Loosening Ownership Restrictions

One could surely wonder how there can be a scarcity of media voices in an era with the Internet, cable and satellite communications, and more radio and television stations than ever before. The issue, however, is not how many outlets exist, but how many owners control those outlets and the ease of access for multiple and distinct voices to be heard. Another factor is whether the voices that are heard are the voices of corporate, financially concerned giants or the voices of citizens wanting to inform and distribute culture to each other. Surely, it is quite challenging for the FCC, academics, and other observers to fully gauge and interpret the ramifications of ownership models in the media sphere, but deliberation is surely needed as policy changes are considered. Having multiple and varying voices in the media market is too critical to the nation's cultural and policy interests to take chances. If the media giants gain even more properties and influence, and federal regulators ultimately determine that wasn't a good thing after all, think of how difficult it will be and how long it will take to dismantle the media dynasties and return media access to a more widely distributed marketplace.

When a divided FCC moved forward with its proposed ownership rules in 2003, Commissioner Jonathan Adelstein issued a vigorous dissent, saying the plan to allow big media corporations to get bigger could "damage the media landscape for generations to come." He went on to say, "It threatens to degrade civil discourse and the quality of our society's intellectual, cultural and political life." While big media forces dismiss Adelstein's "sky is falling" rhetoric, if he is right and the deregulatory agenda is implemented, the damage would have already been done with little prospect for repair.

A former media big shot himself, Ted Turner now warns that big media corporations don't serve communities effectively. In an article in *Washington Monthly*, Turner wrote that big media companies are concerned only with profit and will run with whatever program materials are cheapest, even when those "decisions run counter to local interests and community values." That means a loss of more expensive local programming, to be replaced by cheaper national programming.

When the FCC announced in the summer of 2006 that it was formally proceeding to rework its media ownership rules, the president of the Media Access Project, Andrew Jay Schwartzman, issued a press statement in which he said, "Over the air broadcasting and daily newspapers are, by far, the most powerful forces shaping public opinion on local and national issues. It is as simple as this: diversity in media ownership is good for democratic self-governance." He is correct, of course. A report based on a Peabody Seminar sponsored by the University of Georgia came to a similar conclusion: "The work of these massive organizations [media conglomerates] touches leisure and education, culture and custom. It affects the distribution of key resources. Most significantly, it affects possibilities for democratic discourse and participation."

Even in a capitalist society, the public's interests must be considered ahead of the economic interests of big corporations. The FCC and the courts should keep that in mind as this extra-inning contest over ownership regulations goes on and on.

# CHAPTER NINE

❧

# How You Can Fight Back—Today

Electronic and print-media producers combine to put a giant footprint on our culture, in terms of both content and tone. The producers and editors of the big media world, after all, have the television and radio airwaves and a million cable channels. They use ink by the barrel. The megacorporations that dominate the media have their hands in the journalistic, entertainment, and advertising sides of the industry. Together, these media biggies determine for us our nation's cultural standards, the agenda for our news discussions, and, generally, what is relevant and trendy in society.

Sadly, too much of the public is complacent in allowing the powerful media to dictate our cultural standards. Other citizens simply feel resigned and helpless to do anything about it. There might not be an actual, declared culture war going on through the media, but there is surely a process underway where the media centers of Hollywood and New York work to define those cultural standards. Although the mass media have the ammunition, access, and power to impose these cultural decisions, the public can and must play an influential role in defining what is culturally acceptable, entertaining, and relevant. The public's power must come from within and be exhibited through a multitude of consistent small gestures that create a cumulative effect that can't ultimately be ignored by the media powerful.

The greatest element the public can use in exercising its voice in the definition of media content is fear. The one thing that scares media producers is the possibility that the audience will desert them. Without audiences, media companies have no advertisers and no money. When the public speaks out about questionable media content, media owners become fearful that the audience could eventually depart. Even on small matters, bad publicity can hurt media companies in the image department, resulting in advertisers with cold feet or worried stockholders.

A culture is defined by the stories it tells to itself, by the topics deemed worthy of discussion, and by the manner in which those conversations take place. The content of our cultural dialogue and the standards in which that dialogue takes place are too important to leave to the whims, greed, miscalculations, and bizarre judgments of media owners and producers who don't understand the values and priorities of the wide majority of Americans. Americans who feel powerless to affect the content and practices of the mass media have given up their collective voices, which, if put to use, could engage the struggle and impact the media landscape. Ultimately, the content and practices we see disseminated through the media will be defined by the standards of regular guys speaking up or by the media elites guiding cultural directions for us.

"Feed forward" is the concept that media producers feed audiences what they think audiences want and need. This process, however, is very unreliable. What are the odds of megamedia power brokers in Los Angeles or New York, walking on red carpets and being chauffeured in limos, being able to understand the entertainment or information needs of the 99.999 percent of the nation that doesn't float around in those circles? Negligible. What is needed is for the audience to step up and make its voice heard in ways that go beyond the media-managed focus groups and surveys.

The fact that so few Americans complain directly to media outlets is interpreted by the media as a sign that the public is generally satisfied with mass media fare. Of course, that is a false interpretation. A survey in *Time* magazine in 2005 showed that large majorities of Americans believe that television contains too much violence, bad language, and sexual content. Many others are disturbed by the manner in which alcohol and drug abuse is presented. Still, the research results showed only 5 percent of Americans had ever contacted broadcasters or the government about their concerns. This defeatist and lackadaisical attitude is quite confusing, given the activism with which Americans normally express themselves. Any local government that contemplates raising the water rates in a community will receive countless complaints and packed city council meetings over the issue. Customers rail to gas station owners every time the price of gas goes up. The returns department of any clothing store sees a steady flow of traffic from customers who don't like the fit, style, or workmanship of a garment they've purchased. But too many Americans sit and take it while media outlets exercise poor journalistic judgments or air program content that is contrary to the public's values. Media performance can change when media consumers change their attitudes on actively providing input to the program decision-making process.

Contrary to what many people might think, it doesn't take mass petitions or thousands of phone calls to prompt change within a media organization. A high-profile television news anchor in one of the nation's largest markets revealed in a background conversation that the management at his station will sometimes alter content decisions or newsroom practices based on the reception of just one viewer complaint. Conversations with other broadcast professionals indicate that this sort of reaction is not so out of the ordinary. This sort of knee-jerk response seems rather irrational, in a sense, but it does demonstrate that media management can be sparked into change by minimal public input. That is caused, it could be argued, because so much broadcast and print material is disseminated that receives no public response. Thus, even a few well-argued responses from passionate members of the public could prompt media managers to pause and ponder.

Even the Federal Communications Commission (FCC) has no threshold for how many complaints it must receive before looking into a possible violation of federal regulations. One legitimate audience protest can prompt a commission review and subsequent penalty against a broadcaster. Indeed, that was the situation when a single complaint to the FCC about George Carlin's "seven dirty words" led eventually to a Supreme Court decision in 1978 regarding broadcast indecency. The FCC is required to look into each situation based on its merit, not based on whether a certain number of complaints are filed.

Some media executives falsely assert that citizens who complain about media performance are somehow un-American and are seeking to dismantle the free speech guarantees of the First Amendment. They claim that public pressure amounts to censorship and oppression of ideas. Public activism to comment on and ultimately influence media content, however, is not an anti–First Amendment gesture. In truth, such activism by the public against institutions of power is exactly the kind of expression the First Amendment was designed to encourage and protect. When members of the public challenge the powerful media on issues of content, professionalism, and so forth, we see a clash of ideas on the direction of our culture. The marketplace of ideas welcomes this clash and supports all parties having a say in the discussion, especially the voice of the citizenry exercising its free expression against the media powerful. Citizen activism into media content is needed to challenge the media establishment. It is not censorship to challenge the collective judgment of the media industry. Nobody is restricting the media industry's right to broadcast and print whatever it wants when citizens stand up and ask for something better and different. Public pressure and social give-and-take comes with the free marketplace of ideas. Media outlets have the right to ignore public sentiment; they just do so at the risk of losing their audience and the financial resources that accompany that audience.

Executives in the media industry will posture that they alone understand the significance of the First Amendment and represent us in its defense. The media industry, however, is more interested in self-preservation and its ability to make money than the concept of free expression or representing average Americans in its application. The so-called Free Speech Coalition would appear to be a civic-minded organization committed to maintaining fundamental rights. In reality, however, the coalition represents and is funded by the adult entertainment industry in order to battle pornography and obscenity statutes around the country. Media consumers absolutely cannot assume that the media industry is looking out for the public's interests or has any inside track on knowing what those public interests are. The media-consuming public must be more proactive in asserting its priorities, interests, and concerns to the executives who make their money by selling audience eyeballs to advertisers.

# Small but Important Ways to Assert Public Opinion to the Media Decision Makers

Media consumers can make a difference in the caliber of the media content that is peddled to them if they would collectively let the industry know more about their likes and dislikes. This need not be a daily effort on the part of audience members, but it does need to be done when a topic or concern grabs your interest. Responsible input on those topics of concern and relevance to the audience needs to get to media decision makers. Otherwise, those decision makers go blindly on with the false assumption that they know what's best for the audience. It's not that hard to do, and every bit of input plays a part in providing the public voice. This public input need not be just for criticism. Audience members need to let media producers know the programs or approaches they appreciate. A more complete dialogue with the media powerful thus includes audience likes and dislikes.

## Go Directly to the Media Bosses

Members of the public who want to provide input on media performance should be sure to take their comments as far up the ladder as possible. If you don't like the manner in which a news story was covered, don't bother telling the reporter; make your comment to the editor of the newspaper or the general manager of the television station. If you don't like how your local deejay performs on the radio, don't call him; contact the owner of the station. If you don't like the tone of a commercial, don't call the station broadcasting it; call the owner or CEO of the company that sells the product. Many media people at the lower ends of the organizations look at public input as self-serving and inappropriate pressure. They are also too close to the content to fairly assess its quality. Most important, however, the on-air people or individual writers at media outlets are not in management positions and thus have less concern for the media organization's public image and business climate. Contact information for the big shots can usually be found on the website of the particular media organization. If you can't get them to pick up their phone, leave a voice mail. Most execs can be contacted by e-mail, of course. If you can't get a direct phone call, voicemail, or e-mail, ask the switchboard operator for the name of the big cheese and then mail your comments addressed to the name of the manager. If you absolutely can't figure out the biggest manager to receive your concern or can't get to that person, at least find the name of the ombudsman for the organization. You need somebody outside of the trenches to have the basic chance to get a fair hearing for your concern.

In your contact to the media biggies, give them as much detail as possible about the broadcast or news story that prompted your message. Do not assume that the manager or editor knows the content of everything that is disseminated by their organization. Explain precisely what it was that you disliked or appreciated and how you arrived at that conclusion. For example, if you think a story was reported unfairly, indicate the standard on which you've made this conclusion. Were both sides not presented? Were facts incorrect? If you think a news story was too sensational, what video or aspects of the presentation were over the top? If broadcast content was offensive, what words or depictions were out of line? Without giving away private details, give the management some context so they know where you are coming from. Let them know if you are a parent and you don't appreciate that your kids saw the troubling material. Let the management know how regularly you watch that station or read that publication. Let them know something about your demographic background—career, location, age, and anything else that might help them understand you. The receiver of your message must know you are a real person and be able to develop a picture of you. The less anonymous you are, the less likely the management is to dismiss you as a nut or wacko. And, of course, don't yell, threaten, or engage in personal attacks. That's a sure way to have a media manager dismiss your concern and chalk it off to fringe status, thus perhaps even having a boomerang effect on the point you are pushing.

Don't use form letters if you want the media organization to take you and your like-minded friends seriously. Form letters are considered the work of self-interested zealots and are easily ignored by media managers as unworthy of consideration. Five original contacts of concern are worth a thousand form letters or mass e-mails. If the matter is important enough to prompt you into voicing your opinion, take the time to telephone directly or send an original e-mail or letter. Taking the easy way out with a systematic, copied complaint letter is pretty much a waste of your effort.

## Take Part in Participatory Media

In this era, most media outlets provide opportunities for viewers and readers to engage the media organizations. So have at it. The obvious avenues are published letters to the editors of newspapers and call-ins to talk radio shows. There are no guarantees that your letter will be published or your call accepted, but it's worth a shot. It helps to get to the point and be civil. If you don't get your letter in on the first try, send another one. Call the radio talk show host until your opportunity arrives. Many newspaper and television station websites have places where readers can comment on a story or even rate it. Take advantage of these quick and easy opportunities to express your opinion. These actions should not be taken in place of direct contact with the media bosses, as outlined above, but they still serve a function.

Many media organizations now recruit and work with reader advisory boards or focus groups. Volunteer to serve on such boards if the media outlets in your community operate such things. They may not publicly advertise for these positions, so be proactive and call the organization to volunteer your services. If you don't get into these discussions, somebody whose input you don't appreciate will, and the media managers will think those people are representative of the community's perspectives.

## Let Advertisers Know What You Think

Activist media citizens need to be in touch with advertisers for two reasons. First, advertisers need to know what you think of the programs they sponsor. If there are programs on radio or television that you believe are inappropriate, make direct contact with the advertisers to let them know your opinions. Let them know what it is about the show that you don't like and that their continued sponsorship affects your image of the company and your purchasing support of it. The radio and television companies provide advertisers with ratings numbers to show how many people are in the audience, but those ratings numbers don't tell anything about the people who *don't* appreciate a particular show. Contacting wayward advertisers lets them know there is at least some repercussion for sponsoring the edgy programs.

The other reason to contact advertisers is to let them know what you think of the actual commercials they are running. Without a doubt, advertisements play a large part in defining the cultural values of our time. The storylines of the commercials, the humor demonstrated, the attitudinal tone, and the imagery shown with the products all say something about how that advertiser views our society and its values. Watch an evening's worth of television commercials and see how many of them show rude behavior, nasty insults, suggestive sexuality, or people being injured. You will see credit card commercials where a guy is constantly being belittled and injured. You will see a beer commercial in which a woman holding a candle in a wagon gets torched by a flatulent horse. You will see a disrespectful and slobby depiction of a guardian angel. You will see a nearly naked woman washing a car and eating a hamburger. You will see a cell phone commercial in which two teen girls are physically brawling. You will see a woman being injured by a fellow airline passenger who repeatedly drops his luggage on her head while fending off another passenger who is trying to steal his ice cream.

Such commercials tell the viewing world that this kind of material is acceptable culturally and for selling products. If you disagree with the approach, let the advertisers know. Most companies have websites with a "contact us" section. Use it to express concern about the content and tone of commercials. The response you get will likely say that the commercial was test-marketed in front of a focus group that thought the message was acceptable. But that focus group was probably made up of a handful of young adults who live on the coast and who don't necessarily represent the nation's overall values. Advertisers need to know the values of regular Americans who don't appreciate sick humor, sleaze, and violence as a way to market products.

Direct input from many regular people is likely more helpful than the occasional high-profile advertiser boycott. Those efforts succeed in generating more attention for the advertiser, which is just what advertisers want. When advertisers are challenged about particular shows being sponsored, the show in question also gets more publicity and, consequently, can pick up new advertisers to replace any that might be scared off by the orchestrated boycott.

## Contact the Government

If you have complaints about indecent content in broadcasting, take your concern directly to the FCC. The FCC has simplified the process for citizens to file complaints. The easiest way to register your concern is at the FCC's website, through FCC Form 475B (http://svartifoss2 .fcc.gov/cib/fcc475B.cfm). The form asks for your name, address, and phone number, and then asks for you to indicate the date, time, and channel of the offending program. There is also a section to provide any details about the program that you care to share. Unlike in previous years, you are *not* required to provide a transcript or electronic record-ing of the broadcast in question. The FCC can order the offending sta-tion to provide those materials for analysis. Of course, if you have the transcripts or recording, feel free to send those to the FCC in order to expedite the process. Each complaint to the FCC is then reviewed to de-termine if further information is needed and, ultimately, to determine if a violation of the FCC's rules has taken place. As indicated earlier, it only takes one contact to put the FCC investigation into process, but the FCC will not begin a review process absent a complaint from the public. The FCC relies on public input to initiate indecency complaints, and it is most rare for the FCC to monitor stations of its own accord.

Citizens should also engage their congressmen regarding concerns about the media world. Congress has the power to impact the media world in many places, including the regulation of advertising, owner-ship limits on media properties, shield laws for reporters, political broadcasting rules, video, games, Internet control, children's television, and so forth. Many of these issues don't come with cookie-cutter, pre-determined party-line directions, so many congressional representa-tives will rely more heavily on what they hear from constituents. The increased fines on indecency violations passed in 2006 were largely the result of high-volume constituent input that went across party bound-aries. Contact your congressmen by phone, by letter, or via e-mail at their websites. Most congressmen have local constituent service reps who travel the district and set up shop occasionally in local courthouses to receive public input. Make your input heard.

Cable television franchises in your area are handled by city govern-ments. Let your mayor and council members know what you think of the cable service they franchise. The city likely has a cable advisory board to oversee the franchisee, and these meetings are open to the public. Attend these meetings to express your comments about cable pricing, cable content, and technical standards.

## Get Media Literacy into Your
## Schools . . . or at Least Your Home

If your school district does not have a full-fledged media literacy program functioning effectively, get parents and other concerned citizens together and work to get such a program in place. A good place to start the discussion is with the school district's curriculum coordinator. Then expand the dialogue to include building principals and whatever parent organization operates in your community. Many school corporations have curriculum advisory committees that include parents and other interested community members. Step forward and volunteer to serve on such committees to make sure media literacy initiatives get onto the agenda. The wheels in curriculum reform sometimes move slowly, but do get the ball rolling and keep the effort visible until progress starts to happen.

Don't expect the school professionals to do your homework for you or to gather the materials you need to make your case. Many professional educators are focused largely on managing their current programs . . . their own priorities. You can find materials to make a case for media literacy at websites sponsored by groups such as the Center for Media Literacy (www.medialit.org), the New Mexico Media Literacy Project (www.nmmlp.org), the Alliance for a Media Literate America (www.amlainfo.org), and the Media Education Foundation (www .mediaed.org). In addition to helping make the case for media literacy education, these sites can provide sample curricula and teaching resources. Other websites can provide ample information about the influence of media and potential concerns of media content: Morality in Media (www.moralityinmedia.org), Media Research Center (www.mrc.org), Parents Television Council (www.parentstv.org), and Media Wise (www.mediafamily.org).

Pull together a few allies to make sure the school district knows your initiative has broad support and isn't the work of just a few antimedia nuts. Recruit some local leaders to support you, including local ministers, some college professors from media studies or psychology or sociology departments, and a couple of government leaders who aren't viewed as overly partisan. If you can get a local broadcast or newspaper owner on board, so much the better, but don't expect him to warm to an initiative that promotes critique and analysis of the media.

Ultimately, you need to get your proposals in front of the school board and get them on the bandwagon. Don't be satisfied or buffaloed if you are told that studying media literacy isn't a core subject and thus the schools can't afford the initiative. What can be more important than understanding one of the most overwhelming and pervasive influences that society imposes on our children? Don't be distracted by explanations that sufficient media literacy study happens on the fly in English or through current events segments in social studies classes. Also, keep in mind that using media in the teaching of other subjects is not a substitute for instruction *about* the media. Unless there are specifically designed learning modules on media literacy, taught by teachers who have some formal preparation in the area, students will not learn effectively about media effects and processes. Finding teachers who are prepared to instruct in media literacy will be difficult, since virtually none of them will have had media studies courses in their college training. Most school districts, however, have funds set aside for teachers to do professional development, and teachers can be provided stipends to attend media literacy workshops or take relevant university classes.

Whatever level of success you have in getting media literacy into local schools, at the very least make sure that media literacy happens in your own home. Use the resources from the websites listed above to educate yourself and then provide a homeschool situation for your own family with regard to the media.

## Manage Your Kids' Viewing . . . and Your Own

There are two keys to effectively managing media consumption—moderation and selection. M&Ms are sometimes fun to eat, but you wouldn't eat a two-pound bag in one sitting or let your kids binge on them. A few are okay, but two pounds are not good for you. It's the same with media usage. Watching an hour or two of television a day is relaxing and enjoyable. Leaving the television on all day as a way to avoid doing anything else responsible is destructive. Moderation is also the key with video games, watching DVDs, browsing the Internet, and so on. Media can't be allowed to take over your daily existence. Let the kids (or you) play a video game for an hour, then find something more productive for them to do. Watch a movie on DVD over the weekend, but not five.

Make conscious decisions about what you are going to watch and then specifically watch those programs. Don't go into the family room to just "see what's on." Use television listings to determine what you want or need to watch. Don't just cruise with the remote control looking for something that might catch your attention. That's a formula for wasting a lot of time, and chances are, you will end up in such circumstances gravitating to the more mindless side of television offerings. Television programmers stopped trying to develop quality programming in the early 1960s and instead developed a strategy of "least objectionable program." With this approach, quality of content doesn't matter. Most people will watch television just to watch television, regardless of the quality of the program. Thus, television programmers only need to provide material that is the least objectionable at a particular time slot. If audiences ultimately will watch whatever is on, programmers figure it is a waste of effort and money to develop quality material. This approach represents a rather dim view of the audience, but the audience has such low expectations for quality that the strategy works.

Don't let a child ask permission to simply go "watch television." Train your children to ask to watch a particular program that they have in mind. If the kid asks to watch TV, the answer should be no. If the kid asks to watch *Sesame Street*, then if all other things are equal, the answer can be yes. Modeling is key if you want your children to develop sensible media habits. If you sit like a blob for hours watching whatever's on, your kids will learn to do the exact same thing.

Although this is difficult in a media-obsessed world, work to keep electronic stuff from being the focal point of your kids' daily lives. Keep televisions and video game stations out of the kids' bedrooms. One or two televisions per household should be plenty. If you have a television in the kitchen or dining area, make a family rule that it stays off during meals. The Internet stations in your house shouldn't be in high-traffic or prominent locations, rhetorically blaring how important they are in your daily lives. They should, however, be in locations where a parent can cruise by and see the screen. Kids don't need to watch a video every time they hop in the van. Don't store your DVDs in plain sight as a reminder of how essential they are. Instead, store them in a closet and visibly display your books where children can symbolically be reminded that the mind can be activated without electronic inputs.

## Technology Can't Be Allowed to Dazzle Us

Clearly, Americans are easily dazzled by the technology associated with the media. They shouldn't be. While the improvements in media technology are impressive from an engineering standpoint, consumers exaggerate the importance of having the latest technology. Young adults parading around with iPods are making statements about how trendy and hip they are. The music being played is a nice touch, but not essential to one's daily functioning. Sure, one can store a gazillion favorite songs, but practically, how many of them does the individual really like or ever hear cycled through anyway? Guys want giant televisions to watch football, then sit a half mile away while watching. College students are so into using cell phones and instant messaging (IM) that they will call or IM a friend who is literally in the dorm room directly across the hallway. Having the latest technology can be a status symbol more than meeting any sensible need. Evidence supporting that point came from a study late in 2005 that showed 49 percent of all people who owned high-definition TV sets weren't actually watching high-def because they were unaware that they needed a set-top hookup to see the programs in high-def. Thus, these people blissfully and proudly watched their expensive high-def television sets with a picture quality no better than their previous sets, and never knew the difference. This technology for technology's sake takes on the tone of Marshall McLuhan's assessment over a generation ago that "the medium is the message."

It is bad enough that electronics manufacturers and technology suppliers bombard us with advertising messages about how badly we need the latest in technology, but we must also deal with politicians who try to convince us of our technology "must haves." In the early 1990s, then vice president Al Gore went about promising all Americans access to the information superhighway. In 2006, House minority leader Nancy Pelosi pushed an agenda that would guarantee every American access to broadband technology. These statements suggest that technology luxuries should become necessities. There's nothing essentially wrong with the spread of such access, but it signifies to the few people who don't have broadband that they are somehow diminished or neglected. But it sounds cutting-edge when politicians can prioritize high tech, and it's easier to promote than access to food, health care, and jobs. Besides, the marketplace will eventually drive technology access across the society, and the politicians can cheerlead and take credit while doing nothing except staying out of the way.

## Ratings Book Holders Have Special Power

Those people who are selected by ratings companies to record their listening and viewing habits in ratings books have a special opportunity to affect the future content of radio and television. Arbitron is the leading company that researches the sizes of radio audiences around the country. Nielsen Media Research is the company that researches television audiences around the country. Both make use of ratings diaries delivered to randomly selected people in each media market around the country. Those people selected are asked to record their media-consumption habits for a week. In addition, Nielsen chooses about five thousand households on a national basis to electronically record that household's viewing on a daily basis. The results provided by these statistically representative respondents are projected to represent the viewing habits of an entire market, or in the case of the Nielsen families, an entire nation.

The power for the families selected to participate comes in the fact that each represents the many families who are not recording their data for the research companies. Given that there are over 110 million television households in the United States, and only five thousand Nielsen families, you can see that each family whose data are collected represents well over twenty thousand families. Thus, if your family is watching a stupid sitcom, Nielsen, the broadcasters, and the advertisers all will assume that twenty thousand other families like yours are also watching that program.

While certainly, those families selected on either the national or local market basis to record their viewing habits should do so as accurately as possible, those families should also be highly aware of the significance of their choices.

## Use the Media as You Choose, Not as the Media Would Have You Choose

Ralph Waldo Emerson once wrote, "To be yourself in a world that is constantly trying to make you something else is the greatest accomplishment." Of course, he wrote those words long before the onslaught of electronic media's power, but they have particular relevance for each of us today in facing the mass persuasion, cultural framing, and information warping provided by today's mass media. The media world today is, indeed, trying to make us something else—more consumer oriented, more trendy, more lax in cultural standards, more insensitive to violence, more out of shape, more of anything that promotes the values of advertisers and big media. If we don't individually and collectively do anything to stop this cultural contamination, we do surely lose the opportunity to be ourselves and instead become the creation of forces "trying to make you something else."

FCC commissioner Michael Copps didn't overstate when he addressed a children's television summit in 2006: "TV, radio, cable and now the Internet are perhaps the most powerful forces at work in the world today. . . . But when they are used to misinform and mislead they can—and do—inflict lasting harm." Each American needs to empower him- or herself with the immunization that becoming more media literate can provide. Take charge of your own media habits. Effectively manage the media habits of your children. Let media managers, advertisers, and government leaders know what you expect from the media products that affect our society. Don't be a blob, a couch potato, or any other kind of media victim.

Media consultant and researcher Peter DeBenedittis sees the potential for a cultural revolution in American media. His website promotes media literacy for "prevention, critical thinking, self-esteem." A message on the site reads, "I see a culture formed around humanity's hearts and desires, not manufactured by commercial greed. I see media and entertainment that expresses, enriches, and enhances, rather than teaches compulsive debt, substance abuse, violence, and risky behavior because there is profit in it. I see a world where everyday people have the power to shape their culture because they have access to the information and communication venues upon which democracy depends." For DeBenedittis's vision to become reality, we all must become media activists and demand that our media outlets serve our interests, not the interests of powerful corporations, advertisers, cultural manipulators, and ideologues. We must shape our media future in a manner that, as DeBenedittis asserts, serves our society and our democracy.

# Bibliography

18 U.S.C. 1464.

Adelstein, Jonathan S. "Press Conference on Fake TV News: Widespread and Undisclosed." Statement on behalf of the Federal Communications Commission, April 6, 2006. www.fcc.gov/headlines.html.

Albarran, Alan B. *Management of Electronic Media*. 3rd ed. Belmont, CA: Thomson Wadsworth, 2006.

Amanpour, Christiane. Speech presented at the Radio-Television News Directors Association's Edward R. Murrow Awards Ceremony, Minneapolis, MN, September 13, 2000. www.rtnda.org/resources/speeches/amanpour.shtml.

Aufderheide, Patricia. *Media Literacy: A Report of the National Leadership Conference on Media Literacy*. Washington, DC: The Aspen Institute, 1993.

Bagdikian, Ben H. *The New Media Monopoly*. Boston: Beacon Press, 2004.

Bartholow, Bruce, Brad Bushman, and Marc A. Sestir. "Chronic Violent Video Game Exposure and Desensitization: Behavioral and Event-Related Brain Potential Data." *Journal of Experimental Social Psychology* (forthcoming).

Benoit, William L., Glenn J. Hansen, and Rebecca M. Verser. "A Meta-Analysis of the Effects of Viewing U.S. Presidential Debates." *Communication Monographs* 70, no. 4 (2003): 335–50.

Benoit, William L., John P. McHale, Glenn J. Hansen, P. M. Pier, and John P. McGuire. *Campaign 2000: A Functional Analysis of Presidential Campaign Discourse*. Lanham, MD: Rowman & Littlefield, 2003.

Bergen, Lori, Tom Grimes, and Deborah Potter. "How Attention Partitions Itself during Simultaneous Message Presentations." *Human Communication Research* 31, no. 3 (June 2005): 311-36.

Berger, Arthur Asa. *Media and Society: A Critical Perspective.* Lanham, MD: Rowman & Littlefield, 2003.

Bliss, Edward, Jr. *Now the News: The Story of Broadcast Journalism.* New York: Columbia University Press, 1991.

Brewer, Paul R., and Xiaoxia Cao. "Candidate Appearances on Soft News Shows about Primary Campaigns." *Journal of Broadcasting and Electronic Media* 50, no. 1 (March 2006): 18–35.

Brown, James A. *Television "Critical Viewing Skills" Education.* Hillsdale, NJ: Lawrence Erlbaum, 1991.

Bryant, Jennings, and Susan Thompson. *Fundamentals of Media Effects.* Boston: McGraw-Hill, 2002.

*Chaplinsky v. State of New Hampshire*, 315 U.S. 568 (1942).

Christakis, Dimitri A., and Frederick J. Zimmerman. "Media as a Public Health Issue." *Archives of Pediatrics and Adolescent Medicine* 160 (April 2006): 445–46.

Christakis, Dimitri A., Frederick J. Zimmerman, David L. DiGiuseppe, and Carolyn A. McCarty. "Early Television Exposure and Subsequent Attentional Problems in Children." *Pediatrics* 113, no. 4 (April 2004): 708–13.

Committee on Communications. "Children, Adolescents, and Advertising." *Pediatrics* 118, no. 6 (December 2006): 2563–69.

Coulson, David C., Daniel Riffe, Stephen Lacy, and Charles R. St. Cyr. "Erosion of Television Coverage of City Hall? Perceptions of TV Reporters on the Beat." *Journalism and Mass Communication Quarterly* 78, no. 1 (Spring 2001): 81–92.

Croteau, David, and William Hoynes. *The Business of Media: Corporate Media and the Public Interest.* Thousand Oaks, CA: Pine Forge Press, 2001.

DeBenedittis, Peter. "Media Literacy: A Science-Based Rationale." Paper posted at www.medialiteracy.net.

*Does Ownership Matter in Local Television News? A Five-Year Study of Ownership and Quality.* Report by Project for Excellence in Journalism, April 29, 2003.

*Do Local Owners Deliver More Localism? Some Evidence from Local Broadcast News.* Report by the Federal Communication Commission, June 17, 2004.

Escobar-Chaves, S. Lilliana, Susan R. Tortolero, Christine M. Markham, Barbara L. Low, Patricia Eitel, and Patricia Thickstun. "Impact of the Media on

Adolescent Sexual Attitudes and Behaviors." *Pediatrics* 116, no. 1 (July 2005): 303–26.

Farnsworth, Stephen J., and Robert S. Lichter. *The Nightly News Nightmare: Network Television's Coverage of U.S. Presidential Elections, 1988–2000*. Lanham, MD: Rowman & Littlefield, 2003.

Farsetta, Diane, and Daniel Price. *Fake TV News: Widespread and Undisclosed*. Report for the Center for Media and Democracy, April 6, 2006. www.prwatch.org/fakenews/execsummary.

*FCC v. Pacifica Foundation*, 438 U.S. 726 (1978).

Fox, Julie R., Annie Lang, Chung Yongkuk, Seungwhan Lee, Nancy Schwartz, and Deborah Potter. "Picture This: Effects of Graphics on the Processing of Television News." *Journal of Broadcasting and Electronic Media* 48, no. 4 (December 2004): 646–74.

Fyfe, Kristen. *Wolves in Sheep's Clothing: A Content Analysis of Children's Television*. Report by the Parents Television Council, Los Angeles, 2006. www.parentstv.org/PTC/publications/reports/childrensstudy.

Gitlin, Todd. *Media Unlimited: How the Torrent of Images and Sounds Overwhelms Us*. New York: Henry Holt, 2002.

*Global Implications of Media Industry Conglomeration: A Peabody Seminar Report*. Athens: University of Georgia, 2005.

Grabe, Maria Elizabeth, Shuhua Zhou, Annie Lang, and Paul David Bolls. "Packaging Television News: The Effects of Tabloid on Information Processing and Evaluative Responses." *Journal of Broadcasting and Electronic Media* 44, no. 4 (Fall 2000): 581–98.

Grossman, Dave, and Gloria DeGaetano. *Stop Teaching Our Kids to Kill: A Call to Action Against TV, Movie and Video Game Violence*. New York: Crown Publishers, 1999.

Hahn, Dan F. *Political Communication: Rhetoric, Government, and Citizens*. State College, PA: Strata Publishing, 2003.

Haiman, Franklyn S. *Freedom of Speech*. Chicago: National Textbook Company, 1984.

Harrison, Kristen. "Is 'Fat Free' Good for Me? A Panel Study of Television Viewing and Children's Nutritional Knowledge and Reasoning." *Health Communication* (forthcoming).

Hentoff, Nat. *The First Freedom: The Tumultuous History of Free Speech in America*. New York: Delacorte Press, 1980.

———. *Free Speech for Me—but Not for Thee: How the American Left and Right Relentlessly Censor Each Other*. New York: HarperCollins, 1992.

Hilliard, Robert L., and Michael C. Keith. *Dirty Discourse: Sex and Indecency in American Radio*. Ames: Iowa State Press, 2003.

Hollihan, Thomas A. *Uncivil Wars: Political Campaigns in a Media Age*. Boston: St. Martin's, 2001.

The Home Technology Monitor. *How Children Use Media Technology 2003*. Menlo Park, CA: Knowledge Networks/Statistical Research, 2003.

Johannesen, Richard L. *Ethics in Human Communication*. 5th ed. Prospect Heights, IL: Waveland Press, 2002.

Kaplan, Martin, Ken Goldstein, and Matthew Hale. *Local News Coverage of the 2004 Campaigns: An Analysis of Nightly Broadcasts in 11 Markets*. Los Angeles: USC Annenberg School for Communication, 2005.

Koppel, Ted. Speech presented at the Radio-Television News Directors Association's Paul White Award Dinner, Las Vegas, NV, April 19, 2004. www.rtnda.org/resources/speeches/koppel.shtml.

Lang, Annie, Deborah Potter, and Maria Elizabeth Grabe. "Making News Memorable: Applying Theory to the Production of Local Television News." *Journal of Broadcasting and Electronic Media* 47, no. 1 (March 2003): 113–23.

Leighley, Jan E. *Mass Media and Politics: A Social Science Perspective*. Boston: Houghton Mifflin, 2004.

Lewis, Justin, and Sut Jhally. "The Struggle over Media Literacy." *Journal of Communication* 48, no. 1 (Winter 1998): 109–20.

Lipschultz, Jeremy H., and Michael L. Hilt. *Crime and Local Television News: Dramatic, Breaking, and Live from the Scene*. Mahwah, NJ: Lawrence Erlbaum, 2002.

Martin, Kevin J. Remarks at the Newspaper Association of America annual convention, Chicago, April 4, 2006. www.naa.org/upload/chairman_martins_remarks.pdf.

McChesney, Robert W. *Rich Media, Poor Democracy: Communication Politics in Dubious Times*. Urbana: University of Illinois Press, 1999.

*McConnell v. FEC*, 540 U.S. 93 (2003).

Meyrowitz, Joshua. "Multiple Media Literacies." *Journal of Communication* 48, no. 1 (Winter 1998): 96–108.

Mindich, David T. Z. *Tuned Out: Why Americans under 40 Don't Follow the News*. New York: Oxford University Press, 2005.

Minow, Newton N., and Craig L. Lamay. *Abandoned in the Wasteland: Children, Television, and the First Amendment*. New York: Hill and Wang, 1995.

Murray, David, Joel Schwartz, and Robert S. Lichter. *It Ain't Necessarily So: How the Media Remake Our Picture of Reality.* New York: Penguin Books, 2002.

Murray, Michael D., ed. *Encyclopedia of Television News.* Phoenix, AZ: Oryx Press, 1999.

Nathanson, Amy I. "Factual and Evaluative Approaches to Modifying Children's Responses to Violent Television." *Journal of Communication* 54, no. 2 (June 2004): 321–36.

National Association of Broadcasters. *Inside NAB: 2005 Annual Report and Member Resource Guide.* Washington, DC: Author, 2005.

———. "Nationwide Poll Finds Broad Approval of Broadcast Election Coverage." Press release, October 29, 2004.

*News Audiences Increasingly Politicized.* Report by the Pew Research Center for the People and the Press, June 8, 2004. http://people-press.org/reports.

Papper, Bob. *Local Television News Study of News Directors and the General Public.* Washington, DC: Radio-Television News Directors Foundation, 2003.

Patterson, Thomas E. *Doing Well and Doing Good: How Soft News and Critical Journalism Are Shrinking the News Audience and Weakening Democracy—and What News Outlets Can Do about It.* Cambridge, MA: President and Fellows of Harvard College, 2000.

"Playing with Kids' Minds?" *Indiana University Medicine,* Spring 2003: 2–4.

Poniewozik, James. "The Decency Police." *Time* 165, no. 13 (March 28, 2005): 24–31.

Postman, Neil. *Amusing Ourselves to Death: Public Discourse in the Age of Show Business.* New York: Penguin Books, 1985.

Potter, W. James. *The 11 Myths of Media Violence.* Thousand Oaks, CA: Sage Publications, 2003.

———. *Media Literacy.* 3rd ed. Thousand Oaks, CA: Sage Publications, 2005.

Powell, Michael K. "Don't Expect the Government to Be a V-Chip." *New York Times,* December 3, 2004.

Proffitt, Jennifer M. "The Question Remains—Can Government Intervention Promote Free Speech? Revisiting Arguments for Structural Regulation." *Communication Law Review* 6, no. 1 (2006): 28–46.

Project for Excellence in Journalism. *The State of the News Media 2006: An Annual Report on American Journalism.* Washington, DC: Author, 2006. www.stateofthenewsmedia.com/2006.

"Review of the Radio Industry." Draft of a report by the Federal Communication Commission, 2003.

Rey, Rut. "The Impact of Live versus Packaged News on Television Viewers' Information Processing of Some Episodes of the Iraq War." Paper presented at the annual convention of the Association for Education in Journalism and Mass Communication, San Antonio, TX, August 2005.

Rideout, Victoria, and Elizabeth Hamel. *The Media Family: Electronic Media in the Lives of Infants, Toddlers, Preschoolers and Their Parents*. Menlo Park, CA: The Henry J. Kaiser Family Foundation, 2006.

Rintels, Jonathan, and Philip M. Napoli. *Ownership Concentration and Indecency in Broadcasting: Is There a Link?* Report by the Center for Creative Voices in Media, September 2005.

Robinson, Thomas N., Melissa Nichols Saphir, Helena C. Kraemer, Ann Varady, and Farish K. Haydel. "Effects of Reducing Television Viewing on Children's Requests for Toys: A Randomized Controlled Trial." *Developmental and Behavioral Pediatrics* 22, no. 3 (June 2001): 179–84.

*Roth v. United States*, 354 U.S. 476 (1957).

Rubin, Alan M., Elizabeth M. Perse, and Robert A. Powell. "Loneliness, Parasocial Interaction, and Local Television News Viewing." *Human Communication Research* 12, no. 2 (Winter 1985): 155–80.

Schauer, Frederick. *Free Speech: A Philosophical Inquiry*. New York: Cambridge University Press, 1982.

Schmuhl, Robert. *Indecent Liberties*. Notre Dame, IN: University of Notre Dame Press, 2000.

Schudson, Michael. *The Sociology of News*. New York: W. W. Norton, 2003.

Sikes, Alfred C. "The Eight Blindspots of TV News Have Left Us Poorly Informed." *Broadcasting*, May 11, 1992: 63.

Silverstone, Roger. "Regulation, Media Literacy, and Media Civics." *Media, Culture and Society* 26, no. 3 (May 2004): 440–49.

Singer, Dorothy G., and Jerome L. Singer, eds. *Handbook of Children and the Media*. Thousand Oaks, CA: Sage Publications, 2001.

Slattery, Karen, Mark Doremus, and Linda Marcus. "Shifts in Public Affairs Reporting on the Network Evening News: A Move toward the Sensational." *Journal of Broadcasting and Electronic Media* 45, no. 2 (Spring 2001): 290–302.

Smith, Craig R., and David M. Hunsaker. *The Four Freedoms of the First Amendment*. Long Grove, IL: Waveland Press, 2004.

Sterling, Christopher H., and John Michael Kittross. *Stay Tuned: A History of American Broadcasting*. 3rd ed. Mahwah, NJ: Lawrence Erlbaum, 2002.

Tedford, Thomas L., and Dale A. Herbeck. *Freedom of Speech in the United States*. 5th ed. State College, PA: Strata Publishing, 2005.

Traudt, Paul J. *Media, Audiences, Effects: An Introduction to the Study of Media Content and Audience Analysis*. Boston: Pearson Education, 2005.

Trent, Judith S., and Robert V. Friedenberg. *Political Campaign Communication: Principles and Practices*. 5th ed. Lanham, MD: Rowman & Littlefield, 2004.

Tuggle, C. A., and Suzanne Huffman. "Live News Reporting: Professional Judgment or Technological Pressure? A National Survey of Television News Directors and Senior Reporters." *Journal of Broadcasting and Electronic Media* 43, no. 4 (Fall 1999): 492–505.

———. "Live Reporting in Television News: Breaking News or Black Holes?" *Journal of Broadcasting and Electronic Media* 45, no. 2 (Spring 2001): 335–44.

Turner, Ted. "My Beef with Big Media: How Government Protects Big Media—and Shuts Out Upstarts Like Me." *Washington Monthly*, July/August 2004: 30–36.

Valentino, Nicholas A., Vincent L. Hutchings, and Dimitri Williams. "The Impact of Political Advertising on Knowledge, Internet Information Seeking, and Candidate Preference." *Journal of Communication* 54, no. 2 (June 2004): 337–54.

Wallace, Karl R. "An Ethical Basis of Communication." *The Speech Teacher* 4 (January 1955): 1–9.

Wartella, Ellen, and Gary E. Knell. "Raising a World-Wise Child and the Power of Media: The Impact of Television on Children's Intercultural Knowledge." *Phi Delta Kappan*, November 2004: 222–24.

White, Ted. *Broadcast News: Writing, Reporting, and Producing*. 4th ed. Burlington, MA: Focal Press, 2005.

# Index

# About the Author

Jeffrey McCall is a media studies professor at DePauw University. He is also a contributing op-ed columnist on contemporary media issues. His columns have been published in a number of newspapers, including the *Indianapolis Star, Chicago Tribune, Milwaukee Journal-Sentinel, Washington Times, Buffalo News, Toledo Blade, Seattle Post-Intelligencer,* and many others. McCall is a widely quoted media observer and critic, having been interviewed and quoted by over seventy-five newspapers, including the *Los Angeles Times, Newsday, Christian Science Monitor,* and others. He has also made a number of appearances on radio and television shows, including several appearances on Fox News Channel's *The O'Reilly Factor.* Before moving into academia, McCall worked in the professional media. His PhD is from the University of Missouri.

P
92
.45
n35